COONHOUND BIBLE AND COONHOUNDS

Your Perfect Coonhound Guide

COONHOUNDS, COONHOUND DOGS, COONHOUND PUPPIES, BLUETICK COONHOUNDS, TREEING WALKER COONHOUNDS, REDBONE COONHOUNDS, REDTICK COONHOUNDS, COONHOUND TRAINING, HUNTING, CARE & MORE!

By Mark Manfield

© DYM Worldwide Publishers, 2019.

Published by DYM Worldwide Publishers 2019.

ISBN: 978-1-913154-09-7

Copyright © DYM Worldwide Publishers, 2019
2 Lansdowne Row, Number 240 London W1J 6HL

Table of Contents

Introduction

T his book will introduce you to the world of Coonhounds and will also serve as a guide to answer all the questions you have about them. What is a coon dog? How do you pick Coonhound puppies? What's the difference between a Blue Tick Coon and a Red Tick Coon, beyond their colors? Which is the best coon dog for you? What does it mean when your coon dog goes treeing? (We will also explain what that is). This book will answer your questions and help you learn what you need to know about Coonhounds, and much more. This will teach you how to choose, adopt, care for, play with, train, and even breed what is considered one of the world's best raccoon hunting dogs.

Redbone Coonhounds have a solid red coat,
with only white around the brisket as permissible.

This book will also tackle unique Coonhound characteristics people find appealing and teach you how to what you should expect from a Coonhound's personality. How do Treeing Walkers behave compared to a Redbone Coonhound? What kind of Coonhound toys will bring out certain behaviors? What is the ideal Coonhound weight? Is it healthy for them to be a stay-at-home dog or one that is active outdoors? This book will also help you extend your Coonhound's lifespan by helping you choose the best dog food for your dog and by identifying the most common Coonhound health problems.

This book also has a Coonhound breeds list, detailing different coon dog mixes as well as Coonhound breeds regulated by the American Kennel Club (AKC). There will also be a lot of Coonhound pictures, so you get to see the different breeds for yourself. Famous Coonhounds like Dunk are also featured here so you can read about them.

Finally, this book will also guide you on how to pick from the different types of Coonhounds, and whether you should try Coonhound adoption as puppies, or buy adult Coonhounds. Having Coonhounds as pets can be a rewarding experience, and this book will help you take care of them, and even train them for AKC Coonhound events.

Why Are Coonhounds So Special?

It is iconic in cartoons to see a dog bark up a tree, its front legs planted on the trunk after it has cornered its prey. Little do common folk know that this is the signature move of the Coonhound and that this behavior is called "treeing." Having been trained to track and tree raccoons, this breed barks, to let hunters know the presence of potential game in the high branches and canopies in the wilderness.

Although we no longer rely on these dogs to find food for us or the iconic coonskin caps of centuries past, these mellow and sociable dogs still make for great game hunting buddies and warm up any household. From prize-winning hunters, to simply man's best friend, a coon dog makes for a great addition to any family.

There are six species recognized by the AKC, and each is detailed here in this book. Each one varies when it comes to measures of strength, speed, stamina, sociability, and determination.

Coonhounds also come in many different shades and patterns, each with distinct temperaments and characteristics. For example, the Treeing Walker Coonhound is smart, brave, and well-mannered, while the American English Coonhound or the Redtick Coonhound is sweet, mellow, and sociable. Treeing Walkers are brightly colored and run very fast, while Redticks are darker and camouflage well, for hunting at night.

Redticks are also scenthounds, meaning they hunt prey with their sense of smell. It is said that they can still manage to track a week-old trail. Their floppy, droopy ears, in addition to giving them an adorable look, helps them find fine prey under the foliage. Having these so-called "cold noses," they were incredibly favored by hunters, with the Treeing Walker being awarded the title of "The People's Choice" by Coonhound owners.

These are only two of the Coonhound types this book will tackle, but whatever your choice, a Coonhound is a good companion. They may have been bred for hunting, but beyond the hunt, the Coonhound is a popular choice among dog owners.

CHAPTER 1

Coonhound Origins:
Where Did They Come From?

For millennia, dogs have been both hunting helpers and companions of humans. However, what makes the Coonhound different from the many dog breeds bred for hunting all over the world through the centuries, is that this breed was started and perfected in America.

You might have guessed by now that the Coonhound got its name from its most frequent prey; the raccoon, a pest to the first European colonists in the 1600s who wished to settle in what is now known as the USA.

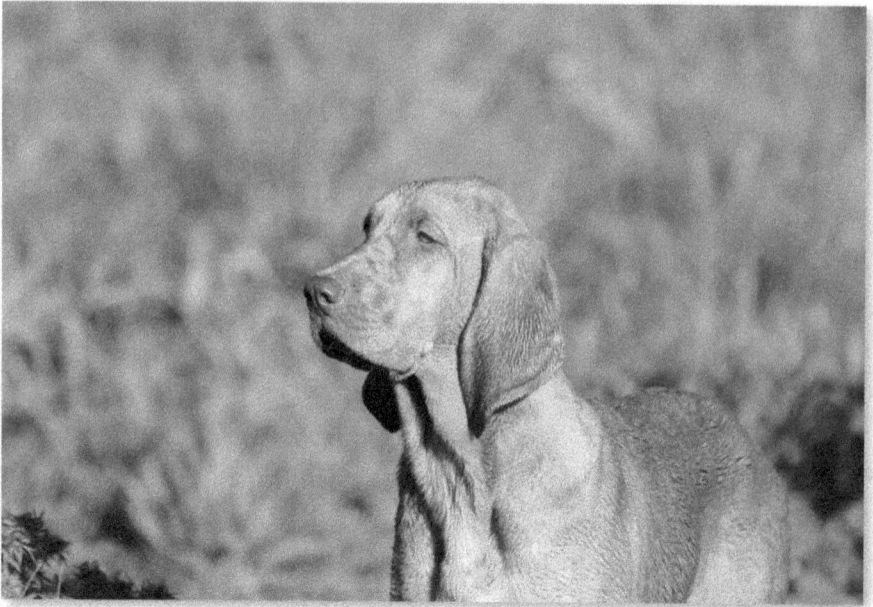

During the early colonization of North America, various breeds of hounds were brought to the new frontier for fox hunting, a favorite sport in that era.

Coonhound History and Origins

The history of Coonhounds is long and colorful. During the early colonization of North America, various breeds of hounds were brought to the new frontier for fox hunting, a favorite sport in that era. These foxhounds, bloodhounds, and other hunting hounds were imported from European countries such as the United Kingdom, Ireland, and France.

At the time, memories of fox hunts in Europe were still fresh in the minds of those in the new world. It also didn't hurt that a few travelers from Europe brought their foxhounds with them. A hunting dog would have been an excellent companion in this wilderness; it was a way to detect the existence of wildlife, whether to trap it for food or to fight it off when it became a threat.

They became so popular George Washington, the first American president, was known to hold fox hunts while riding on horseback occasionally.

However, the first known records of Coonhounds didn't appear until 1860. These were made by Dr. Thomas Henry and Col. Larry F. Birdsong who became the first to keep records to track the performance and maintain the peak abilities of their coon dogs.

Coonhound Bloodlines

The Coonhound was bred from two different breeds: the foxhound and the bloodhound.

Foxhounds were adept in tracking prey. As pack hunters, they would either expect their human masters to trail behind them or leave them behind to catch the prey by themselves. These were suitable traits when the horses of their masters weren't carrying much with them.

The foxhounds would track their target through scent and chase it until the prey was caught or fled to its den where it would be trapped. However, being used to pursue foxes, the breed was known to become confused when its prey ran up the branches of trees.

The bloodhounds were useful in tracking criminals and missing people. After being provided a sample scent, this breed would be able to track the smell of its quarry. The bloodhound was the dog to bring when the prey didn't leave any visible clues or tracks. However, the breed was not without disadvantage, although their ability to follow a scent was desirable, their slow speed and patience hindered the hunt. They also needed a sample scent before they began the chase, without which finding the quarry could be quite challenging.

In a stroke of genius, breeders decided to crossbreed foxhounds and bloodhounds. The resulting breed had the foxhound's speed and determination to chase its prey and corner it, and the bloodhound's ability to pick up the trail as old as three days and track down its source. As a bonus, the breed also exhibited the foxhound's pack mentality and the bloodhound's docility, making for a sociable, friendly, and well-mannered pet.

Over time the descendants of that breed grew to adapt to low light, developed a more musical bark, and learned to lean onto the tree that its prey had climbed up to signal its masters.

Eventually, the Coonhound would branch out to six established breeds: The Black and Tan Coonhound, the Bluetick Coonhound, the Redtick Coonhound, the Treeing Walker Coonhound, the Redbone Coonhound, and the Plott Hound.

These breeds were first recognized by the United Kennel Club. The first Coonhound breed to be officially registered was the Black and Tan Coonhound in 1900. The Redbone Coonhound followed shortly in 1902. The third breed to be registered was the Redtick Coonhound in 1905. The Treeing Walker Coonhound and the Bluetick Coonhound breeds, originally considered English Coonhound variations, were later recognized as separate breeds in 1945 and 1946. The Plott hound was also registered with the UKC in 1946.

What Were the Coonhounds Bred For?

When the English pilgrims first came to Colonial America, they weren't prepared to deal with flora and fauna of the new world, needless to say, they were also ill-equipped for tracking and foraging. While hunting dogs were available, they were not used to the new environment either.

Their misery was compounded by local animals like foxes and raccoons. The latter, in particular, were notorious for their ability to hide in the foliage. They were also smart and stealthy enough to sneak into campsites and settlements and break into food stores or eat cultivated plants.

Early attempts to catch and kill these vermin told the settlers they needed to smell them out since they were well camouflaged in the trees and bushes. And so, the first Coonhounds became the solution to the hunting challenges of the colonists.

While the dogs were used to locate foxes, raccoons, and other animals that posed as either food source or threat, they became famous for chasing and cornering raccoons up the trees, giving rise to the name "Coonhounds."

Coonhounds in Popular Culture

Coonhounds are prominent in American culture, but they aren't given their due. Watch any modern film that features a farm in the countryside, and you will see them being portrayed as dogs just snoozing and lazing away their lives on the front porch. This is the exact opposite of what the Coonhound is known for. The good news is they are done more justice in classic literature pieces and films.

The fictional novel "Where the Red Fern Grows" by author Wilson Rawls revolves around the training for two Redbone Coonhound hunting dogs. The beloved Disney character, Goofy, is said to be a Black and Tan Coonhound. Smokey, the school mascot for the University of Tennessee, is a Bluetick Coonhound. The sequel to "Old Yeller," "Savage Sam," featured a Bluetick Coonhound as well. Famous country songs also featured this breed as well, like George Jones' "Ol' Red."

Art has also paid homage to this breed with art dating back to the late 1800s. One of the most prominent works was made by Glenn Gore named "Treed Short," a fine-line art depicting three Coonhounds having cornered a raccoon up a tree. Another known art piece made by renowned artist Raymond Pease also featured Coonhounds. The art was featured in an illustrated hunting dog book published in 1964.

Coonhounds in the Present Day

While they still being used for hunting, the Coonhound is now more popular as a household pet. Starting in the 1900s century, Coonhounds began to garner appreciation in and around the home. It was also around this time when the Coonhound breed began to spread all over the world.

As dog shows became more and more popular, so did the Coonhound gain a reputation as a show dog. The internet has also contributed to their rising popularity as well as their image of a dog that embraces a healthy and active lifestyle.

CHAPTER 2

Coonhound Breeds & Variations: Which Exist?

H ere are things to keep in mind in considering whether you want to get a Coonhound as a pet, show dog, service dog, or hunting dog. It will also teach you about the standards of coon dogs in the official AKC Registry.

Coonhounds as Pets – Are they suitable?

All dogs are suitable as pets, as they were bred to co-exist with humans and have near-unquestionable loyalty. However, all dogs also have instinctual habits that may prove challenging for the owner to have in a house. As a reminder, we cannot stress enough that pets are a responsibility. Also, dogs are living creatures given to habit and instincts; one should avoid trying to change their behavior drastically, even if you can.

Coonhounds are hunting dogs. They communicate well with humans but have internal hunting instincts.

Coonhounds are hunting dogs. They communicate well with humans but have internal hunting instincts. Going back to the iconic image of them barking up a tree, this is why they chase squirrels and tend to seek locations of optimal vantage, like a couch. They can sniff food and pests with ease and are often fixated on the prize until it is obtained, or they are physically obstructed.

It is also in their genetics to bark at potential threats and prey, as they have developed a mutual understanding that humans will follow their bark, and they get a share of what food is derived from the encounter.

Having such an impulsive, loud, and energetic dog may prove a chore when you want some peace and quiet, not to mention that adults can come close to 80 lbs. (36.2 kg). Coonhounds need an outlet for their incredible skillset, so activity is required. Long walks, frequent playtime, and possibly another dog to socialize and run around with, are things to consider as daily requirements once you have a Coonhound. If you can't afford another dog, dog parks are an excellent way to give your Coonhound the company and activity it needs to stay relaxed and in shape.

If you can't maintain such an active lifestyle, it may be best for you to find a more relaxed dog or have someone help you. Beyond these, a Coonhound is a playful, loyal companion, that provides a lot of affection and protection.

Purebred Coonhound Standards – AKC Coonhound

The AKC describes each Coonhound breed as sociable, easy-going hounds at home, but stubbornly determined during the hunt, during which it performs with high speed and endurance. Its body is streamlined and has no chunky or exaggerated areas. Their walk is described as rhythmic and without effort.

However, the most emphasized qualities in the AKC is the dog's ability to be both brave, and friendly.

Coonhound General Appearance – Coonhounds have a sleek, athletic build. Often domed, their heads are broad and of moderate length. Their ears flop down and often almost reach their noses, but no longer than that. Their necks are muscular and are also of moderate length. Their muzzle is usually squarish, and have flews covering the lower jaw. Their jaws must have a scissor bite, where the lower jaw aligns with the upper jaw so that teeth mesh together cleanly. Their elbows are where their chest ends, and depending on the breed, they come in either three or fewer colors.

Coonhound Size – Each breed is described as at least 25 to 27 inches (63.5 to 68.8 cm) in height, with females being an average of two inches shorter. From the back of the head to the nose is a fair 9-10 inches (22.8 to 25.4 cm). The measurement from the breastbone to the back of its thighs should be a similar length to its height. On its hind legs, a Coonhound can reach roughly four feet high.

Coonhound Weight – While some breeds are larger than others, the average weight of a Coonhound is close to 65 lbs. (29.4 kg). Larger breeds like the Black and Tan can be as massive as 100 lbs. (45.3 kg). or more without looking overweight.

Coonhound Coats – According to AKC standards, Coonhound coats, or body fur, are short and thick, with the Plott Hound sometimes having a second layer of fur. Some breeds have smooth, clean fur, while others have a harder, rougher texture.

Coonhound Temperament – The AKC needs a Coonhound never to be timid or cowardly. Varying amounts of aggression and friendliness are dependent on the breed, but Coonhound bravery is the defining factor of the breed.

Coonhound Colors – Each Coonhound breed is given a specific set of colors that define them as that species. Variations and mutations of the colors are frowned upon and are often cause for disqualification.

Black and Tan Coonhounds have a ratio of black to tan where black must be dominant but not obscure the tan. The tan marks must only appear near the eyes, muzzle, chest, toes, and rear end. Any white mark that is at least one inch long is cause for disqualification.

American English Coonhounds have white fur with red and blue ticking, with red being more common in this breed. Any solid color that has no ticking for at least 10 percent of the dog's fur is cause for disqualification.

Bluetick Coonhounds have black fur with blue ticking, with some tan markings over the eyes, cheeks, chest, and tail. Red ticking also forms on the legs. There are no problems if the tan or red is missing, but the existence of any other color is a cause for disqualification.

Treeing Walker Coonhounds have black, white, and tan marks. Black or white can be dominant, but the tan must only be a trim. The absence of black or tan is not uncommon. Other color combinations are causes for disqualification.

Redbone Coonhounds have a solid red coat, with only white around the brisket as permissible. Darker shades of red around the muzzle are expected, but not required. If there's a whiter mark that can be covered by a hand or any white "stockings," it's a cause for disqualification.

Plotts have it more lax, as any color combinations in the brindle (their coat coloring pattern), is allowed. Even a solid black coat cannot disqualify a Plott, but dark fur colors over light colors are preferred.

Ticking is defined as a special fur pattern that exists in many dogs where a supposed dominant color appears in a white base coat. These little dots of color are so important in some breeds that a dog may be disqualified from contests if any solid color appears in more than a tenth of the dog.

Black and Tan Coonhounds have a ratio of black to tan where black must be dominant but not obscure the tan.

Coonhound Breeds and Distinctions

Black and Tan Coonhound

The Black and Tan Coonhound is the pioneer of the breed. Resembling their ancestors, the closest, they have a keen sense of smell and endurance that pushes them through night hunts, as this is what a Coonhound was bred for.

Named after their color, Black and Tan Coonhounds are covered with short charcoal black fur, with rich tan areas around their eyes, muzzle, chest, rear end, and legs. Some of them develop white areas, usually around the chest, but this is considered undesirable in dog shows.

They are very social, and are protective of their owners, even being brave enough to fight off or hunt larger predators, like mountain lions and bears. They are also powerful, agile, and alert.

This breed is good with children as they are patient and not dominant. They will do anything to sleep next to the people they love, even if space is constricted. It should be noted they become less playful, the older they get.

Treeing Walker Coonhound

These are the descendants of the English Foxhounds that the pioneers brought to the newly-discovered America. The Treeing Walker Coonhound was perfect for the job it was bred for; treeing and hunting raccoons. Also known as "The People's Choice," these dogs are favorites among Coonhound owners.

The breed was named after Thomas Walker, one of the pioneers in the mid-1700s. He mixed the Walker Foxhound with a previously unpopular breed called the Tennessee Lead. This gave this dog a "hot nose," meaning the Treeing Walker could follow a fresh trail in comparison to one that is days old, leading to more successful hunts.

This mix also gave the Treeing Walker its "tall beagle" look. The iconic black and tan over white for this Coonhound can come in other permutations, but these three colors are expected. Having white or black as dominant shades, and sometimes lacking one of the other colors is still beautiful but having a fourth color can make it a flawed breed. Until 1945, the Treeing Walker was considered a subspecies of the American English Coonhound, so some ticking is also not uncommon.

While having powerful legs for the chase and the ability to track its prey up a tree, the Treeing Walker is best known for its looks. Those who own one are often captivated by its default sweet face and pleading expression.

This breed is also safe to have around a family, even its smallest members as they are known to enjoy the company of children.

Redtick Coonhound

It was first called English Fox Coonhound, then the American English Coonhound, before being finally called the Redtick Coonhound. This breed is a mix of the English Foxhound and many other breeds. Over time, it focused more on night hunts.

It was its special coloring that finally gave it its name; this breed has spots of red fur in its areas of white and in other non-white areas. The areas that aren't white may be a shade of black, blue, or more red.

This breed can sometimes sport a brindle pattern while their jaws can also be prone to having an overbite or underbite. Brown, stripe-like patterns, or a misaligned jaw on the breed aren't part of the AKC standards of this breed.

The Redtick Coonhound is described to be sweet, mellow, and sociable, even as it looks gracious, confident, and powerful. It is also one of the fastest breeds of Coonhound dogs.

Bluetick Coonhound

Primed and eager for the hunt, the Bluetick Coonhound needs constant activity to maintain its overflowing reserves of energy, and sometimes this can be too much for some to handle. Therefore, it may not be suitable for first-time Coonhound owners.

When not in the hunt, this dog will grow very affectionate, looking for attention from those it loves. This may lead to some of the more haunting parts of this dog; it's almost mournful marks and howls.

As opposed to the Treeing Walking Coonhound, the Bluetick is known for its "cold nose." It can pick up trails that are many days old. Despite its ability for speed this breed is also known for its dexterity, it is never clumsy.

Much like the American English, the Bluetick is known for its ticking. This dominant blue dotting over its white layers is what the breed is named for. In fact, until 1946, the Bluetick was considered a sub-breed of the American English.

Redbone Coonhound

In the world of Coonhounds, the Redbone Coonhound is considered neutral in many ways. They are a balance of most traits the other breeds are known for; they have a healthy measure of endurance, speed, power, and determination for the hunt. Their less competitive and less aggressive natures make them an easier breed to handle if it's your first time with a hunting dog.

This also means that a mature Redbone can feel at home with toddlers and even other animals. Although the drive to hunt prey is still there, it's more adjusted and adapted to life indoors than the other Coonhound breeds.

This breed is also the kind that cries out if it feels lonely, so it's best suited for an active lifestyle or a protected one inside the house along with members of the family. However, a little of both is ideal.

Its lineage is possibly of Irish ancestry, which may explain the lush red coat the breed is named after. Sometimes some white patches develop near the chest and toes, but it also has the chance to grow unwanted "stockings."

Plott Hounds

While Plott Hounds are classified as Coonhounds, they have no real connection to Coonhounds, or the English foxhounds brought over from Europe. They were bred and raised from Hanoverian Schweisshunds in 1750 by a German in North Carolina, name Johannes Plott.

They were first used for bear hunts, and Johannes' son Henry Plott would later breed more for local stock, solidifying their status from personal mix to a full-fledged breed.

Plotts aren't as fast as the other breeds of Coonhounds, but they make up in strength and determination what they don't have in speed. They are also the most difficult to train, since their ancestors were independent hunters, and need more activity than other breeds.

If you can handle the daunting task, the Plott is a wonderful hunting dog to own. However, you should also know that the Plott hound is the one most susceptible to animal aggression due to its courageous nature. It is not recommended as pets for families with toddlers or very young children, but children over 10 or those who are aware of a dog's boundaries, should do fine.

Some Plotts have a double coat, making them good waterdogs, and helping them through colder climates. The brindle coloration is iconic to Plotts, though sometimes other colors can appear as stripes along their coats. Some white or grey can also appear on the chest and legs.

Coonhound Personality

In general, Coonhounds need a lot of activity to relax, and they bond towards a strong Alpha personality, usually the owner. They are also affectionate. When not hunting, a Coonhound will bond with its owner, often requiring the attention of you or your family members. They get lonely rather easily.

Coonhounds are also loud. They have a melodious but sometimes irritating bark. Often expressive of their emotions, these dogs try their best to communicate to its human or those around it, unmindful of the societal limits of the noise it makes.

Coonhound Behavior

Because Coonhounds are hunting dogs that hunt raccoons and large game primarily, they are brave and have the instinct to explore their surroundings. This bravery can also manifest as aggression and curiosity, depending on the threat it perceives from what it sees. They would typically investigate noises, smells, and new creatures.

They can also get annoyingly stubborn once they start tracking and may even ignore you when you call them.

During a hunt, Coonhounds also know that they have allies with them who can do more in the hunt while they chase. So, they will do everything to alert their allies that they have picked up a scent or cornered a quarry.

Coonhounds tree their prey with persistence. After it has climbed up to the branches of a tree, the Coonhound will not rush off to find another prey item to pursue. It will lean onto the tree they have cornered the prey into and bark until it gets the attention of its master.

Coonhounds can also develop nocturnal schedules because many of them were bred for raccoon hunting, they adapted to when raccoons are most active and tend to be active in the late evening.

Coonhound Life Expectancy

A happy, healthy Coonhound may live as long as 13 years, or even more. They reach that through proper exercise and a healthy diet.

Coonhound Hunting Dogs

Coonhounds have no problem performing as hunting dogs because they were bred for the hunt. However, you should remember that even dog skills need practice to keep them sharp.

With proper training, they can start the hunt on a signal, choose which prey to find, and scout the area of potential threats, like larger game.

Like humans, dogs will also get tired the more they engage in physical activity. Be sure you can identify when your dog is at its limit.

Coonhound Service Dogs

Coonhounds need a lot of training to be a service dog. While their strength, loyalty, and pleasantness cannot be questioned, they may have too much external drive and energy.

When Coonhounds get a whiff of potential food or prey, they will have to resist the urge to give chase. They also have to be able to calm down whenever prey does appear. Take note that while they are capable of suppressing these urges, they must have the outlet they need to focus on the owner's tasks at hand.

Coonhound Show Dogs

During dog shows, Coonhounds only need to behave, show no fear, and have the necessary colors in their fur. Obedience training, good experience with strangers, and cleanliness are the only special actions needed.

For a healthy-looking dog, your Coonhound will need a healthy diet. Make sure they get their protein and plenty of clean water. Weight matters and balanced meals also help maintain their fur's luster.

Coonhound Guard Dogs

Coonhounds make ideal guard dogs because they are brave and protective. Once accustomed to living within the pack that is your family, its barks will be directed at creatures and people other than you and your kin. They are also willing to attack larger creatures, even humans if the threat becomes persistent.

The loud barking of a Coonhound is designed to get the attention of its owner. Given how they have no regard for the noise they make this makes them ideal for securing houses, properties, and even neighborhoods.

Coonhounds and Other Pets

Just like getting used to children, a Coonhound needs to be accustomed to the existence of another family pet. It may take time, but the message will eventually sink in that that animal is part of his pack; a Coonhound will know that you protect certain animals in the family.

However, be warned that its hunting instincts can still be triggered by wild animals and animals from outside the household. It may get used to your dogs, even your cats, but there is no guarantee a neighbor's cat will get the same treatment without the time to get used to them.

Is a Coonhound the Best for Your Family?

There is no doubt that a Coonhound will make for a good family pet. A strong bond is forged in the family a Coonhound lives in, and it will do what it can to keep the family safe.

Still, it is important to remember that hunting dogs need a lot of exercises and maybe a handful without the proper training. It's also advisable to educate your family members, especially the younger ones, about how to keep themselves safe around large dogs.

Popular Coonhound Names – Male and Female

When choosing a name for your Coonhound, it is best to stick to shorter names that the dog can easily remember or react to, when called. The name should be no more than two syllables. A short name is also advisable since you will be using that a lot, especially during training. Remember, that the name will eventually become the equivalent of a command.

Popular names for male Coonhounds:

* Barney
* Bert
* Blue
* Drake
* Duke
* Ford
* Rocky
* Slick
* Sparky

Popular names for female Coonhounds:

* Belle
* Della

- Gracie
- Mandy
- Pearl
- Pepper
- Princess
- Sophie
- Stormy
- Tilly

CHAPTER 3

Buying Your Coonhound Puppy: What Should You Expect?

Before you can even start taking care of a Coonhound, you first need to know where to find one. For first-time buyers or pet owners looking for one whether it's over the internet or in your area, city or state, can be daunting. The good news is there are many sources and a multitude of breeders out there who can provide you with a puppy or full-grown Coonhound.

What are the essential things that you should consider before getting yourself a Coonhound puppy or a dog? What are the right questions to ask breeders or sellers to ensure that you go home with a healthy puppy or adult Coonhound? How much should you expect to spend on a Coonhound puppy or adult?

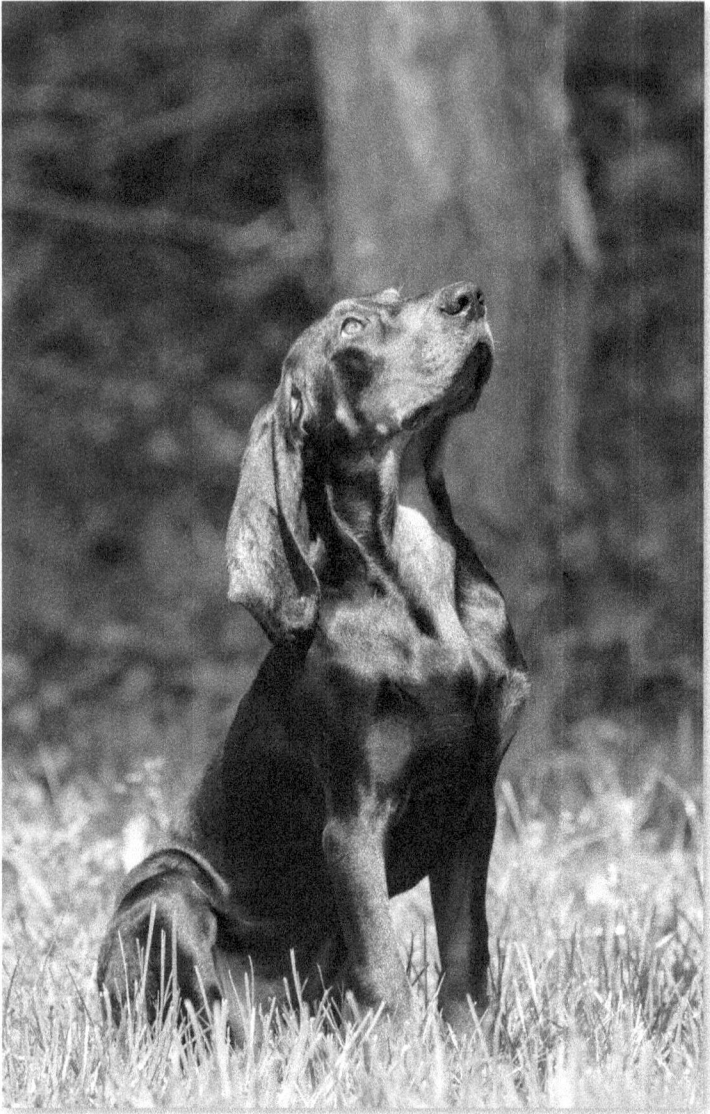

Coonhounds need a big environment for them to roam free and have a healthy life.

Things You Should Consider Before Buying

It might be tempting to buy one immediately, but before you do you should be aware of the following:

You should never agree to have your Coonhound shipped or delivered to you. It is essential that you see the puppy or adult dog you want to buy first-hand. Nothing beats your intuition when it comes to selecting your very own puppy or adult Coonhound. This allows you the time to check the overall health of the puppy as well as ask the breeder as many questions as possible for a thorough background check. This will also help you verify if the seller or breeder is genuine. Be sure to pay on the day (a small deposit before is OK), and never send them the full amount in advance.

Coonhounds need a big environment for them to roam free and have a healthy life. Are you sure you can provide them with this? You may want to reconsider having a Coonhound if you live in a small house or an apartment, with no open spaces. Places such as a big lawn or open parks should be ideal for your growing and developing Coonhound.

Make sure only to buy puppies that are at least eight weeks of age. Coonhound puppies are usually weaned by the time they reach eight weeks old. At this point, they may be able to take in solid foods and would no longer need to feed on their mother.

Coonhound Puppies – Where Should You Look for One?

There are many ways for you to get a Coonhound. Most breeders nowadays would advertise over the internet. But other reputable breeders would be easy enough to find if you know the right people. An excellent place to start is with groups for dog lovers in your local community. These groups often share information on reputable sellers/breeders. You can also check your local

🐕 39

newspaper. You can also find various online groups that focus on specific Coonhound breeds. Social media can help you out with this. If you aren't comfortable with an internet search, you can go ahead and check out your local pet stores, although it pays to do some research beforehand. It would be more advisable to go for a reputable seller or breeder.

The American Kennel Club is also a good group to ask when it comes to reputable Coonhound breeders since it is the official organization for purebred dogs. They have strict guidelines when it comes to registering purebreds. AKC also provides a venue online for breeders to connect with prospective buyers. You can reduce the risk of getting a "fake" Coonhound if you focus on sellers/breeders registered with AKC.

Last but not least, the local animal shelter is also an excellent place to look, you never know if they happen to have a Coonhound up for adoption.

Checking a Prospective Coonhound Puppy – What Are the Questions to Ask?

Once you have found a reputable seller/breeder, you should ask them the right questions about any puppy you want to buy. Reputable breeders are always keen on answering questions from prospective buyers and will not shy away from hard questions.

What qualities the puppy was bred for – First, you may want to ask the breeder what sort of qualities they are breeding for in their dogs. Having the right qualities for your Coonhound will determine if it is the right fit for you as a pet owner. Good-tempered dogs are usually a sign that they have been bred well.

You should also ask the seller/breeder if it's possible to see the location where the Coonhound puppy was raised. With that, you should be able to determine if the location has a suitable environment for raising a puppy. It should be clean and spacious.

If you can, you should also ask to see the parents of the puppy. Both parents should display the qualities that you are looking for. Both should be well-fed and healthy. They should exhibit a caring and attentive attitude towards the pups.

What health conditions the puppy may have or likely develop – It would also be very beneficial to ask if the parents of the puppy have any pre-existing health conditions. This is because genetic defects such as heart problems, orthopedic problems, and the like can pass down to the offspring. Congenital disabilities in Coonhounds are sporadic unless inbreeding occurs.

Ask if any vaccinations and deworming is needed for your Coonhound puppy. Visiting a local trusted pet clinic and consulting a veterinarian would be the best course of action. Have the Coonhound puppy go for a general check-up to see if any existing conditions are present.

What the puppy's diet should consist of – Finally, ask for the type of diet given to the dogs of the seller/breeder. It would be useful to copy the kind of food given to the Coonhound, especially in the early months.

Coonhound Price – How Much They Usually?

According to the AKC:

- A typical Black and Tan Coonhound puppy or adult would usually cost you between $300 to $400. Redtick puppies or adults are around the same.
- Plott Hound puppies or adults cost between $300 to $500 (£230 to £383).
- Treeing Walker puppies or adults cost between $400 to $600 (£306 to £460).
- Bluetick Coonhound puppies or adults cost between $500 to $600 (£383 to £460).
- Redbone Coonhound puppies or adults cost between $600 to $800 (£460 to £613).

Remember that these are only average costs. Some puppies or adults of certain breeds can fetch as much as $1,600 (£1,227) if it comes from a reputable breeder with high-quality Coonhound breeds. During the United Kennel Club's Autumn Oaks event in Richmond in August 2014, some of the Coonhounds were priced at as much as $4,000 (£3,067).

Costs Associated with Raising a Coonhound

A dog, the size of a Coonhound, will cost you around (£38) per month for food or about $600 (£460) yearly. This is if you use grain-free kibble. This diet is more expensive but should be better for your Coonhound.

Necessities such as toothbrush, toothpaste, shampoo, toys, and treats will cost you $35 (£26) a year at this time of writing. Note that shampoo made for humans does not work well for dogs and could cause irritation. Look for organic natural products free from sulfates and artificial colors. You also don't need to go for expensive brands or labels of dog hygiene products. Go for something practical yet cost-effective that helps you budget but still have quality products for your Coonhound.

Annual vet check-ups and vaccinations are a must. Such medical expenses would cost you around $132 (£101) yearly at this time of writing. This does not include flea and tick prevention medicine and heartworm prevention medication which would cost you about $145 annually.

Taking care of a Coonhound can be costly especially if you want them to be healthy and live a long life. Prospective buyers should be responsible and know the costs of having a great dog. Spending a little more for your future family member makes it all worthwhile in the long run!

The good news is that you don't have to spend on everything. A few things can be done to save a dollar or two. For instance, you won't need to pay for a dog walker or dog daycare. You can opt to do this yourself. It will also be good for you to walk your dog daily. In the end, both you and your pet will benefit; you get exercise, and your pet gets bonding time with you.

Also, if you're going on vacation, you can opt not to bring your Coonhound for boarding at the plane kennel. You can have your dog stay with friends who also have dogs, while you are away. Just make sure that your dog is well-acquainted and adjusted with that friend, and that friend's dogs before planning any long out-of-town engagements.

Coonhounds need less maintenance when it comes to their fur than many breeds. Make sure to feed them well and keep them clean. A trip to the dog groomer may not even be needed. You can learn the grooming techniques and procedures by yourself so you can do it at home, this way your dog will feel much better being pampered in familiar surroundings than an alien one.

Dressing up your Coonhounds with dog outfits is an expensive luxury. You won't need this sort of thing unless it's just something you want to do. Also, make sure that your Coonhound is comfortable with wearing clothes, as some dogs don't like the extra weight of unfamiliar overalls, and types of cloth, on top of their fur.

At this point, you now know how to go about buying a Coonhound and how much it may to own one. You can now confidently find yourself a seller/breeder. Please note that sometimes it may take you a bit of time to find a reputable one. You may have to go out of your way and have a long drive to see one. But don't worry; finding the right seller/breeder makes a secure investment for your home and family. It's more important that you buy a healthy, lively, and even-tempered puppy or adult Coonhound.

CHAPTER 4

Coonhound Adoption:
Is It A Good Idea?

What's a better idea than buying a Coonhound? Adopting one instead.

It's a win-win situation for you and the dog; you will only get to spend a fraction of the cost it would take you to buy a dog, and a dog gets a loving forever home with you.

When considering adoption, keep in mind that the best Coonhounds to adopt are those in the shelters who no longer have owners to take care of them, those that were abandoned or abused, and those that were given up willingly or unwillingly.

Coonhound Rescue – What Common Abuses Do They Suffer?

Coonhounds are wonderful dogs to own; however, the sad thing is that not everyone, even those who have spent a lot of time with them, sees their value beyond being mere hunting tools or assistants.

When considering adoption, keep in mind that the best Coonhounds to adopt are those in the shelters who no longer have owners to take care of them, those that were abandoned or abused, and those that were given up willingly or unwillingly.

What is the most common abuse with Coonhounds? Abandonment.

According to the media, in the counties of Halifax and South Boston, both in West Virginia, Coonhounds wandering without owners, becomes a common sight right after hunting season each year.

Not only are these Coonhounds without homes and scared, but most of them are also often found malnourished and in poor health, often diseased and flea ridden. Some even have open injuries and signs of deliberate maltreatment. It's not just the old dogs that can no longer hunt that are abandoned, and there are also younger ones, usually part of a dog party that is rented by professional hunting clubs just for hunting and then discarded after that.

However, despite all this, even those dogs themselves haven't given up hope that people will help them like in the case of a Bluetick Coonhound found wandering the main street of Hurtsboro, Alabama, after she was abandoned by her owner in 2008.

If it weren't for a veterinary clinic receptionist and a postal worker who gave her food when they happened to see her, she would likely have died. Like other Coonhounds abandoned after hunting seasons, she was in poor shape.

While others reason that hunting, dogs are skinny by nature, rescue workers say this particular dog was barely skin and bone when rescued.

"This Coonhound was barely able to walk but was still wagging her tail at people who passed by her. Her front teeth were worn down, probably from trying to chew out of a kennel, and her neck was scarred from wearing a collar that was too tight. This dog still trusted people and was looking to them for help," said a report at the time.

The good news is that this particular dog, who was later renamed Blue Bell, was eventually rescued, rehabilitated, and re-housed.

The bad news is not every abandoned Coonhound ends up like Blue Bell.

Coonhound Rescue – How Can You Help?

If you happen to see a Coonhound that appears to be abandoned or in need of help whom should you contact?

Is it not always a good idea to approach a Coonhound whom you suspect might be abandoned. While on the one hand, the dog might be looking for humans for help, it might also have been traumatized by human contact and treatment.

Be sure you know the signs that a dog doesn't want to be approached; it will stare at lot, snarl or growl, and carry its tail high and move it stiffly from side to side. Remember that a hostile dog will not necessarily assume a combative stance; a dominant, aggressive dog will give no sign before biting.

Your local animal welfare authorities are most likely the first to be able to respond, so they should be the first to be called. Please see your bonus Coonhounds resource chapter at the end of this book for many useful links of Coonhound rescues.

If the dog does appear to be friendly and is receptive to being helped you should first contain the dog and take it to a place from where it cannot get lost, escape, or wander off. Check the dog for tags, as these may have the dog's name and even the owner's address or contact number. If the tags do not have this information, you should take the dog to a veterinarian to scan for a chip.

If you can contact the owner, then there's no more need to contact the authorities. However, if no owner information is found, then you should contact the groups mentioned above.

Adopt a Coonhound

You might have heard it before; adopt, don't shop. It might sound cliché, but it's a good slogan for a good reason.

According to the National Council on Pet Population Study and Policy, approximately 7.6 million companion animals enter animal shelters every year. Of that number about 3.9 million are dogs, and of that number only 1.6 million are adopted into permanent homes. That's less than half.

Take note that just because a Coonhound, or any dog for that matter, is in a shelter doesn't necessarily mean it was abandoned or abused. Some dogs end up in shelter for a number of reasons like being on the receiving end of a terminated marriage, being left behind after the death of their owner, being given up because the owner lost his or her home, being given up because their owner can no longer train or take care of them, or merely because they got lost or separated from their owner.

Most importantly, it also doesn't necessarily mean that a shelter dog is a bad dog.

Coonhound Adoption – What Should You Consider?

Your mindset – You might become quickly overcome with pity after reading the plight of a rescued Coonhound and look to adopt it immediately. However, this feeling might disappear over time, leaving you with a dog you suddenly realize you no longer care about, and the dog with an unreliable future ahead. Make sure you have the right intentions when you adopt a rescue animal; and that is that you want to adopt that dog because you want that dog to have a better future and you are in a position to provide that.

Dog advocates would say it similarly: Adopt a rescue dog not because of what happened to it in the past; adopt it because of what you can provide for it in the future.

Your patience – Do you have the patience to deal with a rescue dog? While abandoned Coonhounds are likely to have interacted with human previously, a dog that has been abandoned for quite some time may have "trust issues" the same way a human does. Trust can be earned over time; make sure you have the patience to give the dog time.

In the case of Coonhounds that were given up because their owners have given up trying to train them, this becomes even more challenging. Are you sure you have the energy it takes to keep pace with a breed like this?

Your space and facilities – We have already mentioned a Coonhound will need a huge space to run around in. This isn't just so they can stay healthy, the activity also serves as an outlet for the dog's energy, without which it might be tempted to bite and destroy things. A rescue dog will need that space, and that activity, to be able to feel like their old selves again.

Your other animals – Already having other animals in your care might be an issue, especially if there are other kinds of dogs. A Coonhound is a social dog and wants to be around other dogs and play with them. Considering how much energy a

Coonhound has it might be a handful for dogs that aren't used to rough play.

Smaller animals may also be at risk. While a Coonhound that has been raised around smaller animals may develop a familiarity with them, this doesn't go for animals it hasn't been raised with. A trained Coonhound will likely look at smaller animals as prey items and will immediately have the instinct to chase them.

Make sure you can get that dog well-acquainted and used to your other animals.

Your family members – Do you have very young children who might get hurt if the dog plays with them?

Your budget – Last but not least you should also consider your budget. Can you afford to take care of another animal, on top of the ones you may already have?

Note: Remember that we said adopting a dog is cheaper than buying one? A Redbone Coonhound puppy will cost between $600 to $800 (£460 to £613) while an adult will cost between $500 to $700 (£383 to £536). However, adopting one will only cost you around $300 (£230).

Coonhounds for Adoption Near Me – How do I Find Them?

Please see a list of adoption resources at the end of this book in the Bonus Chapter.

CHAPTER 5

Coonhound Care: How Can You Ensure A Healthy Coonhound?

Y ou've wanted a Coonhound for so long, and now you finally have one. Now, what do you do?

Raising A Coonhound – Do You Have What It Takes?

As with raising any pet commitment is critical.

A pet is a source of joy as well as a responsibility; you can't just buy one and leave it alone, while it begs and begs for your attention.

*Think twice about getting a Coonhound if you can't promise to spend
a lot of time with it or to readily provide what it needs.*

Yes, it's true some animals are low maintenance; you buy them
and practically give them space until they come to you when
they need something, or you realize that they have specific needs.

However, the Coonhound isn't one of those pets. It will need constant attention and care. It will also require more of your time than regular pets.

Think twice about getting a Coonhound if you can't promise to spend a lot of time with it or provide what it needs.

If you can't promise these but still want a Coonhound that is active and happy, then you better have someone who can make the needed provisions.

Coonhound Puppy Care – What Are the Important Things to Remember?

Again, it's important to get puppies at eight weeks old, this way they are ready to be separated from their mother.

Getting a Coonhound when it's at a young age has its advantages:

- You get to control the environment it grows up in
- It can grow up with and get used to the animals, people, and children around you
- You can teach that puppy from scratch what kind of behavior you want from it

The first time you come home with a puppy allow it to relieve itself in your designated potty area. That way it already has an idea it should do its business there. If the puppy isn't ready to "go" yet, let it sniff around your house to familiarize with its surroundings until it shows signs it's ready to "go."

Never let it out of your sight as it explores its new home. This is also an excellent time to talk to the puppy, to let it get used to the sound of your voice. You should also start calling the puppy by its new name.

You should already have prepared a sleeping area for the dog, in the puppy's case a dog bed, or blanket, in a small dog crate.

All dog owners know the first night or nights with a puppy is always the toughest, the poor thing will whine and howl for its mother and littermates. You might be tempted to take it to bed with you, but don't; this will encourage negative behavior from it later on.

Note: There is something you can do to alleviate this anxiety. Before you go to where you pick up the puppy, bring a plush toy with you. Get the scent of the puppy's littermates (or better yet, the mother) on the toy and bring it with you. When it comes time for the puppy to sleep, give it the toy to snuggle with. Dog owners have reported this has worked wonders alleviating the anxiety puppies feel in a new environment.

For the first week or two, it's advised to have this crate just near your bed, that way you can take the puppy outside to the designated potty area, in case it shows signs it wants to "go."

Over time you can move this sleeping area to another area in the house, then outside the house, eventually.

The puppy's first few days in your house should be quiet and calm. It is adjusting to its new environment after all. Don't worry, the Coonhound in it will come out soon enough.

After the worst of the whining and howling is over taking care of a Coonhound puppy will be like taking care of a puppy of any dog breed for the first few months.

Establish a routine – With young dogs it's important to establish a routine, set a time for when you feed the dog and make it regular and consistent. This also goes for exercise and playtime.

Designate different areas for different purposes – Make sure the puppy knows that different areas have different purposes, one area is for eating, one area is for sleeping (although it doesn't hurt to put its food bowl near its crate), one area is for exercising, and another area is for relieving itself. That way it will learn not to play in the sleeping area or relieve itself in a non-designated area.

Make sure it eats well – A Coonhound puppy requires four meals a day until it is four months old, from there two meals a day will suffice. Again, everything should be set to a regular schedule so your dog will have a grasp of different times during the day.

One thing you have to realize about Coonhounds is they aren't known for their obedience. They are stubborn by nature, so positive reinforcement goes a long way in training Coonhound puppies. At what age should you start training puppies? The expert said they could be receptive to simple orders as early as five weeks. However, since we advised to get puppies at least eight weeks old, it's better to start training them as soon as they have grown accustomed and comfortable to your house and environment. Start with the basic commands every dog out there should know; "sit," "stand," "shake," etc.

Because Coonhounds fall into the medium or large category, they grow more slowly compared to other breeds. Most of them won't reach their full-sized frame until 15 to 18 months old, and their full adult weight until they're about two years old.

Coonhound Adult Care – Common Practices

Getting a Coonhound as an adult also has its advantages:

- An adult dog will have settled into its personality
- You will have detailed information on its behavior and how it relates to people and kids
- You will have detailed information on its health profile, diet, and exercise regimen

If you are worried about a Coonhound not being able to adjust being transferred from one home to another there's no need to worry; they are capable of to a new location, and even a new owner, as long as they receive more or less the same care and are exposed to the same general environment.

When you bring an adult Coonhound into your house for the first time, let it sniff around and get familiar with the surroundings. While you should be more lenient when Coonhounds are puppies as where you allow them to go, you should teach them to respect boundaries as they grow up, this doesn't apply to adult Coonhounds. Be sure it understands where it can and cannot go, and you have to indicate with precise words and orders like "no" or "down," if it cannot enter a particular room or climb on certain furniture. Don't let it out of your sight while it explores.

If you happen to have children or other animals in the household, make sure the dog understands this is part of their pack. Correct its behavior immediately if it starts to get aggressive with other animals.

As with puppies, make sure it has a designated sleeping area, for adult dogs a crate with a dog bed is also ideal.

While a Coonhound can adjust to living inside as well as outside a house, it would be most beneficial for a Coonhound to live in a dog kennel or crate outside the house, that way it can get to run around and exercise whenever it wants. However, during the cold months, or if the weather is particularly bad or hot, you can move the kennel or crate inside your house.

By now the dog already knows how to tell you it needs to do its business, but if you install a dog door, it can go outside to relieve itself without relying on you to open the door.

Adult Coonhounds should be ready to go for walks as soon as they have settled in; chances are they will be begging for it. Make sure to leash your dog and take it on a route you are familiar with. Let it sniff around and explore, this is a new place for it after all, but you should always be in control of the dog during its first time in an unfamiliar environment.

Take note that you can buy adult Coonhounds that have undergone basic training for coonhunting (started dogs), those that are considered qualified or fully-trained to already start coonhunting (finished dogs), as well as those that didn't undergo training at all (so you can be the one to train them from the start).

An adult Coonhound should be ready to start with coonhunting training immediately after it has gotten used to its surroundings and environment (that way it knows how to find its way home). The training itself will be discussed in another chapter.

When purchasing a Coonhound that has already been named, should you keep a Coonhound's old name or give it a new one? The choice is yours, but the dog will eventually learn to recognize a new name given to it if that new name is used often enough in conjunction with commands and positive reinforcement.

Coonhound Exercise – How You and Your Dog Can Keep Up with the Regimen

We have mentioned this a lot in the previous chapters; a Coonhound will need a lot of exercise to keep fit and stay happy.

As with feeding, you should establish a routine with exercise time, this way your dog will know what to expect and at what time of the day.

After the first few "calm" days to allow your puppy to break in, start walking your puppy, this way it can get used to your environment. Puppies will not require rigorous exercise right away; they are still growing after all. Short daily walks followed by some gentle playtime, will do.

After it reaches six months old, you can now introduce it to its adult routine, which is ideally a daily hour-long walk, followed by half an hour of playtime. Expect the dog to eventually become rowdy, during playtime.

During walks always remember to keep your dog on a leash. Coonhounds are likely to get excited and run off when they see or sniff prey. While they are trained to return to owners (if started or finished) after losing the smell of prey, they can quickly get distracted and get lost.

During long walks don't worry about exhausting your dog. Coonhounds were bred to run for miles. If your dog happens to get tired before you do, then either you are a super athlete, or there is something wrong with your dog.

Playtime need not be the same every time keeping it varied is encouraged (otherwise your dog will get bored). You can switch between playing fetch with a frisbee, running around with a ball, or even just letting your dog chase water from a hose. You can also make up games of your own for your dog.

You may have guessed by now, exercising your dog means you have to exercise as well. However, this is a situation that benefits you both; you both get a good workout, and you get to bond as well.

Managing Coonhound Shedding

Your dog will shed hair, it's not a matter of if but when. There are things you can do to minimize falling hair from a dog:

Brush your dog – This is explained in detail in a later chapter about dog grooming.

Prevent itching – Some hair falls off a dog naturally. However, a lot of hair can also fall off due to scratching. If your dog scratches more than usual, find out what is causing your dog to itch, and help them find a cure.

Feed your dog high-quality food – These foods should have high-quality protein and essential fatty acids.

Give your dog a supplement – If all else fails, supplements that have a lot of thiamine and biotin can help.

Clean up – Yes, this is part of the process. The more regularly you clean up after your dog, the less of a mess it will be. Invest in a good vacuum cleaner; it's more practical than a broom and dustpan.

CHAPTER 6

Coonhound Health: How Can You Ensure It And Reduce The Likelihood of Issues?

L ike humans, dogs may develop health problems as they grow up and grow older. Be sure you know what your Coonhound is likely to suffer from, and how to remedy it in many cases.

Coonhound Health Concerns – What Are the Common Problems for This Breed?

Hip dysplasia and eyelid abnormalities are the major issues with this breed. Coonhounds can also have other concerns like heart disease, and thyroid disease.

*Coonhounds can also suffer from
cardiovascular-hematological-respiratory problems like Blastomycosis.*

They can also suffer from skin diseases and bacterial infections. Because they have long, heavy ears, they can also be prone to ear infections and ear hematoma.

Coonhounds can also suffer from problems like Blastomycosis (a fungal infection which causes flu-like symptoms and skin irritations). They are also known to suffer from gastrointestinal problems like megaesophagus and bloat, and dental problems like prognathism (undershot jaw) and brachygnathism (overshot jaw).

Persistent Pupillary Membranes (PPM) may also occur in Coonhounds. The PPM exists as a blood supply for the lens in mammal fetuses, but sometimes this membrane remains as strands of tissue across the eye even as the dog grows older.

Some can also suffer from Coonhound paralysis, which will be discussed in detail later in this chapter.

Cherry Eye – What Are the Signs Your Dog Is Experiencing This?

Cherry Eye is what exactly it looks like, a cherry or sphere in your dog's eye. This is actually a disorder classified as a nictitating membrane and can happen in cats as well as dogs. In dogs, these often appear in those under two years of age.

This disorder is actually caused by a third eyelid. A third eyelid is common among many species, its role is to supply oxygen and nutrients to the eye by producing tears.

This third eyelid can be turned inside out with detachment, but when the retinaculum which is responsible for anchoring the gland to the periorbita fails, this can result in the gland to prolapse and protrude from the eye as a red, fleshy mass that looks like a cherry.

Cherry eye can self-correct over time. However, it can also be solved non-surgically by simply massaging the affected eye with a downward diagonal movement toward the snout. However, if this persists, there are also some medications and antibiotics which may alleviate symptoms.

Surgery to correct a cherry eye involves the replacement of the gland by anchoring the membrane to the orbital rim. Removal of the gland itself is not advised as it was found to result in reduced production of tears.

Dog Allergies – Symptoms and Treatment

Just like their human companions, dogs can also have allergies. They can get this from pollen, ticks, and other sources.

You should take notice if your dog starts itching, scratching, biting, and chewing more than usual. They can also scratch a particular spot until they develop what is called a hot spot; red, moist, irritated, and some oozy skin lesions. Hair also tends to fall off a hot spot, making your dog look unsightly.

You can treat dog allergies by taking simple steps:

Wipe down your dog after walking – This can remove allergens like pollen on its body which it picked up outside.

Use a hypoallergenic shampoo – Sometimes the cause of an allergy can be an incompatible shampoo. Make sure you use something that doesn't cause itching. Products with ingredients like aloe, oatmeal, or evening primrose are highly recommended.

Give your dog supplements rich in Biotin or Omega-3 – Vitamins for dogs will be explained in detail later in this chapter.

Try giving your dog Sulfodene treatments – This is a proven cure for hot spots and other skin irritations.

Use a medicated spray for allergies – It's better to ask your veterinarian for this one.

Canine Hip and Joint Dysplasia – What Is It and How to Treat It?

Hip dysplasia is a deformity of a Coonhound's tibia. Usually, this doesn't become evident until the dog is six months old. This is more common in Redbone Coonhounds than other breeds.

This can be caused by both genetics (this is more common in larger dogs than smaller ones) and as well as environmental factors like excessive growth and exercise routine, whether the dog is getting too much or too little of it.

Your dog's diet can also contribute to hip dysplasia. If your dog is obese, it can put too much stress on its joints.

Another problem is luxating patella, or dislocation of the kneecap, which becomes noticeable when the dog is between four to six months old.

The symptoms of both include: Decreased activity, decreased range of motion, difficulty or reluctance in jumping, running, or climbing stairs. Your dog might also experience lameness in the hind end, "bunny hop" while running and lose thigh muscle mass.

Depending on the severity of the deformity, a veterinarian can suggest a non-surgical or surgical solution.

Non-surgical treatment involves weight reduction to take the stress of the hips, avoiding hard surfaces during exercise, physical therapy, and taking of non-steroidal anti-inflammatory drugs.

The surgical option will involve the following procedures; Double or triple pelvic osteotomy, Femoral head osteotomy, and Total hip replacement.

Coonhounds are notorious for just gobbling up their food without eating it, the consequences of which can be obesity.

The best way to prevent hip dysplasia is to screen breeding dogs for the deformity.

Coonhound Paralysis – Treatment

This disease has been observed quite a lot in Coonhounds, and it was given a formal name; acute idiopathic polyradiculoneuritis. While the cause of this disease is believed to be raccoon saliva, particularly when the dog's ventral roots and spinal nerves react to it, in rare cases, has also been observed in dogs with no exposure to raccoons or their saliva at all.

This disease begins as a weakness in the rear legs that rapidly progresses toward the hip, resulting in a limp-symmetric paresis.

Within three to four days that paralysis could spread to the rest of the dog's body.

So, if you observe some weakening in your dog's hind limbs, or if you notice it dragging its limbs behind it, you should start to be wary.

If the signs are persistent take it to the veterinarian. It should be the veterinarian to decide if the case can be treated at home or in an animal hospital.

If home treatment is prescribed, ready a soft bed for your dog since it will spend most of its recovery time lying down. Turn the dog over every three to four hours to avoid pressure sores, and provide water close by. You may need to feed it by hand during the recovery period and help it up to relieve itself.

The treatment prescribed is often a mix of detoxification and supplements. Be sure to always coordinate with your veterinarian about the situation of your dog.

Sometimes it takes two to three months for the paralysis to stop, and up to six months for your dog to be back to its old self again.

Coonhound Vaccinations – Which Should Your Dog Get?

Get your Coonhound the following vaccinations against the following diseases; these are what veterinarians would recommend for any dog:

- **Adenovirus** – This can potentially lead to liver disease (hepatitis) and kennel cough in dogs. Make sure to vaccinate your dog against type 1 and type 2.

- **Canine Coronavirus** – This is a dangerous and contagious intestinal disease is spread via feces.

- **Canine Parainfluenza Virus** – This is illness can appear early in dogs, it is also contagious. Your dog should receive a shot against this disease every three years.

- **Distemper** – The dog equivalent of measles, your dog can get this disease from either the saliva of an infected dog or just breathing air sneezed or coughed from it.

- **Ehrlichiosis and Anaplasmosis** – Both are transmitted by ticks. The former is a disease that causes flu-like symptoms in dogs, the latter causes lethargy, fever, and loss of appetite.

- **Leptospirosis** – A disease that can cause internal bleeding and meningitis.

- **Lyme's Disease** – Cause by ticks, this disease can cause lameness, fever, lethargy, and enlarged lymph nodes in your dog.

- **Rabies** – Transmitted through saliva, this virus affects a dog's brain and spinal cord, turning it dangerous and aggressive. Eventually, it will no longer be able to recognize its owner or other previously familiar animals. This virus is particularly dangerous because it also affects humans.

Coonhound Vitamins – Which Should You Give Your Dog?

According to the American Kennel Club, the vitamins dogs need are the same vitamins humans must have. The difference is that dogs need them in different quantities.

Vitamin A – Like in humans, Vitamin A improves dog's eyesight, growth, fetal development, immune functions, and cell functions.

B vitamins – These are vitamins like biotin, folate, niacin, pantothenic acid, riboflavin, thiamine, vitamin B-6, and vitamin B-12.

Niacin, Riboflavin, and **Vitamin B-12** help in the normal function of enzymes.

Thiamine is responsible for regulating energy and carbohydrate metabolism, it also activates ion channels in neural tissue.

Like Thiamine, **Biotin** also metabolizes fat and carbohydrates, it also keeps the dog's coat healthy and helps maintain the functions of the dog's nervous system.

Folate helps a dog's body produce cells, DNA, and other genetic material.

Pantothenic acid is necessary to produce blood cells and also helps in metabolism.

Vitamin B-6 is responsible for glucose generation, red blood cell and nervous system function, hormone regulation, immune response, and gene activation.

Vitamin C – This serves as an antioxidant in dogs, it destroys free radicals in the dog's body, helps reduce inflammation, and helps in the production of brain cells. While dogs can actually produce their own Vitamin C from their own liver, giving them more is good for them.

Vitamin D – This vitamin contributes to your dog's bone growth by letting it balance minerals like phosphorus and calcium.

Vitamin E – This vitamin helps in the development of your dog's eyes and muscles. It also defends against oxidative damage.

Vitamin K – Like in humans, this vitamin helps clot a dog's blood to prevent bleeding.

Choline – This helps maintain a dog's cognitive and liver functions. This is often used to treat dogs suffering from epilepsy.

Coonhound Weight – How Much Should You Feed Your Dog?

The truth is there is no one feeding method, routine, or scheme that can be used as a template for all dogs. This is because for a particular dog's diet there are many factors involved like:

- Your dog's weight and size
- What type of dog food you want to give to your dog?
- How many times a day you feed your dog?
- How much exercise your dog is getting?
- Your dog's metabolic rate

It is recommended you talk to your veterinarian about how much you should be feeding your dog taking into consideration the factors mentioned above.

Note: Coonhounds are notorious for just gobbling up their food without eating it, the consequences of which can be obesity. There is something you can do to prevent this; place a bunch of rocks big enough not to be chewed or swallowed, into the dog's bowl.

This will force the dog to eat its food around the rocks, hence more slowly.

Coonhound Diet and Nutrition – What You Should Know

The most important fact when it comes to your Coonhound's diet is that they require a balanced diet with all of the necessary nutrition components. However, some of these are required more than others, as well as in different amounts.

Puppies will need a diet rich in protein, unsaturated fats, and carbohydrates. As the dog grows up training, dog treats may also make up a huge part of its diet, this is okay as long as it is paired with balanced meals.

Adult Coonhounds will also need a diet with a lot of protein, carbohydrates, and fats if you want them to be active. If you want your Coonhound to more laid back and more of a home dog, you need to get food that isn't rich in fat, to prevent it from gaining weight. Go for a food with a high animal protein content and avoid foods with high grain, wheat/corn content.

Many Coonhound owners to tend to rely on commercial diets in feeding their dogs. This is advantageous since the food is already prepared, and your dog gets food that has been approved by experts. However, you should also be warned that not all commercial food is good for your dog.

While you should also refer to the nutritional label on your dog's food, there is really no guaranteeing that that guide is accurate.

This should also come with a warning; some of the commercial foods are mixed with other low-quality products.

Because of this, it pays to do a bit of research. Read dog food reviews, consult other dog owners online.

CHAPTER 7

Coonhound Supplies: What Do You Need?

Y ou have to have the right supplies to raise, train, and keep your Coonhound healthy. Here are some of the things you will need and advice on how to choose them.

Coonhound Dog Food – What to Consider When Buying

As mentioned in the previous chapter, fat is good for dogs. This is to maintain their health and keep that shiny coat. Fat also supports Coonhound's digestive and liver functions. One ingredient you want your dog food to have is fish oils because these are a good source of healthy fats.

*Coonhounds aren't particularly picky when it comes to dog beds,
but as a responsible owner, it's your job to make sure your dog
is as comfortable as possible when it's resting.*

Aside from fat, your dog will also need proteins and
carbohydrates. So, good dog food should have a combination of
fats, proteins, and carbohydrates. Look for high animal protein,
and low grain content (so not much wheat, corn, etc.)

75

Coonhound Beds – How Should You Choose One for Your Dog?

Coonhounds aren't picky when it comes to dog beds, but as a responsible owner, it's your job to make sure your dog is as comfortable as possible when it's resting. The more rested it is, the healthier and more active it will be.

Consider the following when it comes to choosing a bed for your dog.

The size of your dog – Coonhounds range between medium to large. Make sure it can fit in the dog bed comfortably.

What position your dog likes to sleep in – Some like to curl up others like to stretch out. What kind of sleeper is your dog?

The size of your dog's crate – It's ideal to be able to have that dog bed in your house as well as outside the house, and by outside we mean in your dog's crate. Be sure the bed fits the floor of the crate without the edges folding so your dog can rest comfortably.

If you prefer a doghouse for your dog instead of a crate having a bed inside, it won't do. Dog experts recommend natural bedding for this scenario instead, particularly long-stem grass hay that is widely available in different parts in the US.

Note: It's good to buy cheap beds if you have a younger dog, it will still grow up after all and will need bigger and bigger beds.

If you have a particularly spoiled dog (and you don't mind keeping it that way), you can also buy a blanket for when your dog wants to sleep on the sofa. A blanket will keep your dog warm as well as prevent its fur from settling on the sofa.

Coonhound Collars – How Can You Find the Perfect Fit?

The collar is important because it allows you to attach a leash to your dog. Other than that, a collar will readily identify your dog as an owned dog even if you aren't around.

The basic rule when getting your dog, a collar is not to give them one that's too tight. They can develop neck injuries if this happens. Make sure you can fit two fingers between your dog's neck and the collar it is wearing, also take into consideration how thick their fur is in this area.

Start getting them used to having to wear a collar when they are puppies, this way they will get used to it, as they grow older. Keep in mind that your dog will grow, so it's best to buy cheap collars until your dog has reached its maximum size.

Note: Once you have obtained a collar you should include a tag that has the dog's name and your address and contact details on it. This will come in handy if the dog gets lost.

This tag should be a backup to chipping your dog. Your dog might lose the tag, but never the microchip. You should ask your vet to place a microchip containing your address and contact details, in case your Coonhound ever becomes lost.

Coonhound Leashes – Ideal Types and Lengths

The leash is important because it allows you to walk your dog safely. The leash should be long enough to let your dog explore, yet short enough to allow you to maintain control, at all times.

Note: As mentioned in a previous chapter, some states and municipalities require that the leash on a dog taken out in public should be no more than six feet long (182 cm).

Leashes can come in different materials like nylon, leather, and metal chain. Choose the kind you want but know the advantages and disadvantages. Nylon and leather are light, but dogs can chew through them given enough time and effort. Chain is strong and durable but can also be heavy and rust over time.

Coonhound Harness – Is This Needed?

A leash is something that you attach to a collar, while a harness is something that goes over your dog's chest and back. Most modern harnesses also have rings where you can attach the leash. While a leash will allow you to control a dog by pulling on its neck, a harness does the same by pulling on the dog's back, hence giving you more control and making it easier on the dog.

If your yard is big enough, or you have multiple dogs and keeping them inside is now a handful, you should get an outdoor kennel, also known as a "dog run."

You should put a harness on a dog (aside from the collar) if you have a particularly boisterous dog that needs your intervention, or if your Coonhound tends to pull or jerk when on its leash.

Coonhound Dog Houses – How Big Should They Be?

The most important thing to consider is your dog's size. Before you buy a doghouse take the following measurements of your dog:

- Its overall height.
- Its length from nose to butt (don't include the tail).
- Its height from toe to shoulder.
- Its width.

From here you can determine the proper-sized house to get for it.

- The height of the doghouse should be at least 25 percent larger (but not over 50 percent) than the dog's overall height.
- The width and length dog of the house should be the same, no more than 25 percent larger than the dog's length.
- The opening of the doghouse should be no less than three-fourths of the dog's shoulder to ground height and should be wide enough to accommodate its width.

Remember that large doors aren't necessary, because dogs can duck to enter a doghouse. Another reason for this is the smaller the door, the better insulated your dog.

Outdoor Coonhound Kennels – Should you go for them?

If your yard is big enough, or you have multiple dogs and keeping them inside is now a handful, you should get an outdoor kennel, also known as a "dog run." Unlike a crate or a doghouse, an outdoor kennel is a fenced-in space, big enough for your dog to run around in. Most kennels come in the form of wire-link walls that you can assemble into an enclosed area, to prevent your dog from escaping by chewing, climbing, or jumping over. Many of them also have retractable roofing that can be put in place to protect the dog against the sun or rain.

While it keeps your dog in a certain area, a kennel can let it see what goes on outside it and you can also see how your dog is doing inside. A dog run is also a good idea because it does exactly that; let your dog run. This way it can get exercise by itself even if you aren't around, and you don't have to worry about it getting into your house and destroying things.

It's up to you and your budget how big you want a kennel to be. Whether you put it in the front yard or the back, make sure to leave enough space for you, your family to be able to use that yard in case of special occasions or emergencies.

The kennel should also be big enough so you can put a doghouse in it, with running room to spare. A kennel cannot provide warmth and insulation, after all.

An important thing to remember is to buy a dog run for the size that your dog will become (unless the dog is already full-size). So, if you are buying for a medium-sized dog, prepare for when it will grow up.

Indoor Barriers – Do You Need Them?

While kennels are for the outside, there are things you can use inside your house to maintain control over your dogs. Coonhounds can be stubborn, no matter how much you tell them to avoid certain parts of the houses, chances are they won't obey you. In that case, the best option is to keep them out of those areas using an indoor kennel.

These are simple barriers that are high enough to keep your dog from accessing certain areas, they also have gates you can open and close. You can buy pre-sized barriers, but some manufacturers can also make them to your specifications.

Installing them in strategic areas and particular chokepoints like narrow doorways, the door to the kitchen, or doors to certain rooms, will make them effective.

Coonhound Travel Crates – What is the Best Size?

Eventually, you will want to take your dog out of the neighborhood (sometimes even out of the city or state) if you want to go coon hunting. For that, you will need a proper travel crate. While the meaning they can be secured with a seatbelt or other forms of fasteners and can protect your dog from any injury in case of a car crash, or if the crate slams into the side of your vehicle.

Consider the following when you choose a travel crate for your dog:

- **Size** – The travel crate should be big enough for your dog to sit, stand, and turn around in, but small enough to keep it secure. The rule of thumb here is that travel crates should be no more than six inches longer than your dog.
- **Style** – Heavy-duty plastic or luggage-grade nylon travel crates are best for car transport. If you have to go by plane soft-sided travel crates are ideal.
- **Safety** – Some travel crates have more fasteners than others to allow you to secure it more safely, choose one that works with the vehicle you want to put it in.

Coonhound Toys – What's the best plaything for your dog?

Dogs love to play! Make sure yours has different kinds of toys you can play with together, or it can use to entertain itself. There are generally four types of dog toys, and it would help to have one of each type:

- **Chew toys** – Dogs have this incessant need to chew, and if you don't provide them with something, they will go out of their way to chew anything, and you won't usually like what happens next. Aside from sparing your furniture and household items, chew toys are actually designed for dog use so you can be sure they are safe for them.

- **Tug toys** – These are toys like braided ropes, plastic bones, and the like. Play with your dog by gently pulling on them in a tender tug-of-war. Make sure your dog doesn't end up turning aggressive, and also mind how hard you pull; you might end up hurting your dog.

- **Fetch toys** – These are toys like balls, frisbees, plastic sticks, and other items that can be thrown away for the dog to retrieve for you. Tennis balls are a famous choice. However, the covering on a tennis ball has been proven to scrape the enamel on a dog's teeth, leading to dental issues.

- **Treat-dispensing toys** – Some toys come in the form of balls and cubes that you can hide or put treats in. Your dog plays with them until it can get to the treat. It's a good way to stimulate your dog's intelligence and reward it as well.

CHAPTER 8

How Can You Be A Savvy Coonhound Owner?

Y ou can't own a Coonhound and not expect any changes in your life. You have to make some changes in your home, in your daily routine, in your budget, and most of all, in you. Don't worry, you will get used to these in time. Here are some things you should know as a responsible Coonhound owner.

How You Can Prepare Your Home for Coonhounds

Whether you are bringing home a puppy or an adult Coonhound, it's important to dog-proof your home. This is good for both your home and the latest addition to your family.

Where exactly does this fit in preparing your house for a dog? It protects your dogs against parasites, ticks hide in tall grasses ready to attach themselves to your dog, as it passes by.

Preparing for Puppies

We have discussed how to treat puppies the first time you take them home. However, we haven't discussed how to prepare your home for them.

- **Wrap your trash properly** – Puppies are always curious, and trash can present a variety of new and exciting smells for them.

- **Stow power cords and cables** – Keep these things out of reach, anything rubbery makes for a good chew toy for pups.

- **Keep your medicines** – Medicines for humans are actually a common cause for pet poisonings each year. Keep them out of reach.

- **Keep chemicals out of reach** – These are another frequent source of pet poisoning. Cleaning agents, detergents, car oil, and other chemicals can actually smell appetizing to dogs.
- **Mind high places** – There may be areas in your house that may not seem high for humans but are high enough to hurt puppies if they fall from them. Make sure they don't get to those areas.
- **Know what houseplants are poisonous to dogs** – Plants like the Sago Palm, Castor Bean, American Yew, and Autumn Crocus may look nice in the house, but they are dangerous to dogs if ingested.

Preparing for Adult Coonhounds

Now just because they are adult dogs doesn't mean they won't act like puppies.

- **Keep breakables out of reach** – You might be surprised how Coonhounds can be agile enough to reach something on a countertop or a table after it has piqued their curiosity.
- **Make the yard escape-proof** – Are you sure the dog won't be able to leave your yard without supervision? Sometimes a dog's curiosity will get the better of it and it might just jump or climb over the fence to see what something is, or it just might be feeling lonely.

  Make sure the dog can't climb over your fence. You should also check your fence for weak spots, there may be spaces even you haven't noticed before or spots of soft earth under it that a dog can easily dig through.

- **Mow your lawn** – Where exactly does this fit in preparing your house for a dog? It protects your dogs against parasites, ticks hide in tall grasses ready to attach themselves to your dog, as it passes by.
- **Tell the neighbors you have a new dog** – It won't hurt to inform them you have one, especially if the dog happens to get free and wander around. They may be on alert if they happen to see a strange dog in the neighborhood without being informed.

Preparing Your Family

In the end, it's not just your home that will have to be prepared. Your family will have to know what to expect as well. It's probably a good idea to tell them there will be changes, including a lot of really loud barking at different times of the day. They also have to be prepared for the shedding and drooling (Coonhounds are particularly known to drool), around the house.

Some members of the family might also be tasked to walk and play with the dog, and this will eat up into their personal time. It will also require a lot of physical effort on the part of these persons.

Your family members should also be warned to keep prized possession safely out of reach. Books, shoes, even electronic gadgets can become chew toys if the dog gets them.

The outside of the house will not be spared as well, expect dogs to dig for no comprehensible reason than to entertain themselves. Garden plots will have to be secured, as well as prized outdoor plants.

Coonhound Dog Crates – Are They a Good Idea?

There really is no difference between a dog cage and a dog crate (some pet owners don't use the word "cage" because it implies negative connotations like imprisonment).

Getting a crate for your dog is actually a good idea. This is where you should place the dog when there is no one around to supervise it, and it can also prevent your dog from escaping. Aside from that, a crate can also become a dog's safe haven and refuge. Dogs have a natural to build a den, in the modern age, the crate can serve this purpose.

Note: Never use your crate to punish your dog or send it there for a "time out." If they go there on their own after they feel they have disappointed you then let them, but don't physically haul them in. The last thing you want to happen is for the dog to associate the crate with punishment and negative thoughts.

Coonhound Dog Beds – Where Are the Best Places to Put Them?

Since we aren't familiar with the layout of your particular house, we can tell you where not to place a dog bed. From there you can deduce where the best place is in your house.

- **Somewhere away from appliances** – Dogs have very sensitive hearing and are likely to become unsettled or scared by strange noises and vibrations.
- **Somewhere near where your family gathers** – Because they love to hang out with you, place their bed somewhere they can easily see the other members of your family.

- **Somewhere warm** – Dogs like to sleep where it's warm, don't put their dog beds near windows or doors to the outside, where a draft might come through.
- **Somewhere it doesn't get in the way** – Don't put the dog bed somewhere people can easily trip on it, dog or no dog.
- **Somewhere they can easily get to their food and water** – Don't give the dog a maze, as much as possible it should be a beeline between the sleeping area and feeding area.

Should you have a different bed for your dog for the inside and the outside? This is advisable, but the choice is entirely up to the owner.

Note: Given how active Coonhounds can be, it may also be advisable to get a bed with a non-skid bottom. Dogs will actually scamper out of bed at a call from you, and a non-skid bottom could mean the bed doesn't slide around.

Coonhound Dog Door – What Is the Ideal Size?

A dog door will let your dog in and out of your house without you having to open the front or back door. You won't realize how useful this is until the dog wants to go about its business, at the same time you also happen to be doing your business.

What's the ideal size for a dog door? Like the doghouse, you have to base it on the measurements your Coonhound.

Measure the distance from your dog's toes to the highest point of its back. The distance from the bottom of the dog door to the top of the dog door flap should be this measurement, plus one inch (2.54 cm). Again, dogs can duck to enter a small opening.

Measure the width of your dog, the width of the dog door should be this measurement plus two inches.

Coonhound Muzzles – When Should You Let a Dog Wear Them?

While there is that perception that a dog muzzle can be cruel, the truth is it's only cruel if you choose the wrong muzzle or muzzle them for the wrong reason. The thing is that there are times when you must put a muzzle on your dog.

Consider the following:

• If you are bringing the dog into a new environment, and you aren't sure your dog won't suddenly turn aggressive

• If you want to groom the dog, but it is constantly nipping at you

• To prevent it from eating dangerous items during a walk

• To make a human who doesn't feel safe around dogs, feel safe

• To allow the replacement of plastic cones (also hilariously known among pet owners as a cone of shame)

Here's how to put a muzzle on your dog. One thing you must remember is to show the dog the muzzle several days ahead. Don't just suddenly bring it out and put it on your dog.

Show the dog the muzzle then give it treats. Put treats in the muzzle and have your dog eat them from there. Do this a few times a day for a few days, your dog will soon associate the muzzle with treats.

After a session of treats and muzzles, spray or spread the inside of the muzzle with something soft it will want to eat like cheese, peanut butter, etc. As soon as it finishes licking the inside of the muzzle, gently secure the strap for a brief moment, then slip it off.

Following the next licking sessions, keep the muzzle on for longer periods of time like 30 second, one minute, three minutes, etc. It will eventually get used to having a muzzle on.

Remember not to make the dog think it is being punished when you put on a muzzle. Accompany the action of putting on a muzzle with words of praise, make up a phrase like "here comes Mr. Snuggles" or something to that effect.

Note: Make sure your dog doesn't use the muzzle any longer than it has to, or up to 20 minutes at most, and no longer. Dogs pant to keep themselves cool. Because they can't open their mouth with a muzzle, they tend to overheat quickly.

CHAPTER 9

Coonhound Training: How Can You Get Started & Succeed?

Before you begin, you must know the five key components in training dogs; trust, positive reinforcement, repetition, patience, and consistency.

A dog won't take commands from you or recognize your authority over it unless it trusts you. That's why it's not ideal to train puppies or dogs until you have gained their trust.

Positive reinforcement comes in the form of compliments, praise, and treats. A dog will know if it has done something right if you tell if it's a "good boy" or "good girl," or if you give it a treat.

*A dog won't take commands from you or recognize
your authority over it unless it trusts you.*

Practice makes perfect also applies to dogs. Repeating doing
something over and over again will constantly improve their skills.

You will need patience over the course of training a dog. Your
dog won't be able to get it right the first time, or perhaps the

second, third, fourth, or fifth time. You have to remember that Coonhounds are stubborn by nature and can be hard to teach.

Consistency means there is a corresponding reward or penalty for any action. If you consistently give the dog rewards for good behavior and call its attention for bad behavior, it will be able to tell what behavior will earn it something good or something bad.

Coonhound Training Supplies – What Will You Need?

- **Clicker** – This is a small plastic box with a metal tongue that makes a clicking sound when you press it.
- **Live Raccoon** – This is for getting your dog used to the smell of an actual raccoon.
- **Toy Raccoon** – This is for when you have to train your dog to find a raccoon in various places.
- **Treats** – This is to positively reinforce good behavior.

About Clicker Training

How does clicker training work? Click when your dog does exactly what you want it to do. When you click, this tells your dog it is doing something right, at the precise time it is doing it. With this, you can tell your dog it's doing well even when you are at a distance.

Before you even begin training you should already associate clicks with treats. Click the clicker then give the dog a treat. Repeat this until the dog has associated the clicker with a treat.

During training, you should include praise with those treats after a click.

Before You Start Training

We have already mentioned Coonhounds are stubborn and may choose to ignore you if they get too distracted. This isn't out of malice, it's just their nature. So, the first thing you have to teach your dog is how to pay attention to you.

Say the dog's name then reward them for the attention they pay you. Repeat this process several times until the dog gets used to it. Make sure the dog makes eye contact. Since dogs are natural predators, they rely on their eyes a lot. If a dog has its eyes on you, then you have its full attention.

Another thing you have to remember is to keep training sessions short, around 10 to 15 minutes per session. Humans get tired eventually whether they are doing something tedious like work, or fun like play, it works the same for dogs. Shorter training sessions will also enhance your dog's concentration and reduce the chance of it becoming frustrated.

Whatever the dog does, remember not to punish it (we will go into detail regarding dealing with negative behavior, later in this chapter). Call its attention and make corrections immediately.

Teaching Coonhound Commands – What are the Basics?

There are a few basic commands all Coonhounds must know, these are useful for everyday life, as well as on the hunt.

*   **Sit** – This command will stop your dog from doing whatever it is doing and just sit. Perfect for when you want to groom them or want to stop them from jumping on you or someone else.

- **Lie down** – This usually is a dismissive command; it tells your dog you don't want them around at the moment. Useful for when you are doing chores or busy, and the dog is pestering you.
- **Easy** – This tells your dog to slow down during a walk. Perfect for when you feel you're having a hard time keeping up with your dog.
- **Come** – This is essentially calling to your dog. Use it when you want to feed it, groom it, bathe it, or just hang out with it.
- **Stay** – This is to tell your dog to remain stationary and don't go anywhere no matter what you do or how long you will be out of its sight and hearing.

Training Coonhounds – What Skills Must It Learn?

A Coonhound must learn how to find and tree a raccoon if you want to take it on hunts eventually. You should only train your Coonhound how to hunt raccoons after you are sure your dog has mastered the basics and can now be relied upon to follow your commands.

The first thing you have to do is get your dog used to wooded areas if it isn't already. Instead of the usual places you take it for its regular walk, start getting it used to areas with lots of trees. Your dog should get used to the sights and smells of a forest if you want to take it on a hunt.

After it has gotten used to a wooded area you should get it used to the smell of a raccoon. Use a caged raccoon to get your dog used to its scent. Hide the cage in various places in the wooded area and tell your dog to find it. At this stage, you can just hide it behind a tree.

After your dog has gotten used to sniffing out and finding a raccoon on the ground, it's time to step up the game. Get the toy raccoon and rub it on the live raccoon to get its scent on the toy. Now you can hide the toy in the branches of the trees in the wooded area.

Note that some trainers prefer to use an actual raccoon carcass for the sniffing out and treeing exercise, but considering that it isn't raccoon hunting season all the time killing one might get you in trouble, not to mention looking for a dead one is a whole lot more trouble, compared to trapping one humanely.

Note: Remember that in night hunts and another sanctioned competition, harming or killing the raccoon will result in deductions, so it's important to train your dog to detect and corner a raccoon, not attack and kill it.

What If None of the Training Works?

There are a number of reasons why this could be happening including the following:

- You may not have as close a relationship with your dog as you think.
- Your dog might not be in the right mindset to learn some things.
- Your dog might seem disinterested in training because of the time of day.
- You might be offering your dog the wrong kind of treats.

Another thing you have to remember is that not all dogs will take the same time to train, so don't be disappointed if you have a dog that's lagging behind others.

What do you do if a dog really seems impossible to train? It's probably advisable to just stop trying to train your dog by yourself and seek professional assistance from obedience schools in your area.

How to Deal with Negative Coonhound Behavior

During the early days of Coonhound breeding and training hitting a dog or causing it pain was fully acceptable. Of course, there was no way for the early settlers and breeders to know (or if they did it was too late) that the violence they inflicted on the dogs would have negative effects on the dogs' temperament, resulting in animals that suddenly turned aggressive or snapped, to use human terms.

The bad treatment also resulted in health problems. The dog would also eventually become untrusting of humans in general as well as other dogs and other kinds of animals.

Nowadays you can't hit a dog without being held liable for animal abuse, nor would you want to. So how do you correct bad behavior in a Coonhound? Experts recommend clapping your hands and calling the dog's name with a commanding tone. The dog will be able to tell your mood just by how you are addressing it. Follow this up with a gentle but firm scolding, usually along the line of "no, don't do that."

As much as possible catch or interrupt the dog in the middle of their "crime." For instance, if you don't want them barking loudly for no reason at all, call their attention in the middle of the act. The same thing applies for when they go through the trash, bite furniture, dig in your yard, etc.

Teaching them not to go after food that's not meant for them can be tricky. If this happens too often, you might have to set up an "entrapment operation" where you have to catch them in the act of eating food that you have arranged for them to "steal."

Should You Allow Your Coonhound on the Couch?

There is actually a lot of debate on this one. One on side people would say it wouldn't do any harm to let the dog on the couch, but some animal behaviorists say this shouldn't be the case.

This is because a dog is a pack animal; it will consider you and any member of your family, as well as other animals in your household, as part of that pack. If you give a dog couch privileges, it will start to think it is equal to, or even above, certain members of the pack. This will lead to territorial behavior, with the dog displaying aggressive behavior when the owner tries to move it off the sofa.

To avoid any confusion in the household hierarchy, it's best to tell your dog to keep off the couch.

Training for Coonhound Socialization

During a hunt, your dog will have to learn to deal with other dogs in a way deemed acceptable by competition standards. Remember that fighting is a scratching offense in sanctioned events, so your dog has to be able to get along with other dogs without turning aggressive. The best way to teach a dog to socialize is to take it somewhere it can interact with other dogs.

The best place for this is your local dog park; there will be lots of space to play in and other dogs to play with. If you don't have a dog park in your area, plan with a friend who has a dog or several for an animal "playdate." Try alternating with going to a friend's place and having that friend come over with a dog or dogs, that way your dog can learn to socialize in different environments and under different circumstances.

Even the act of walking your dog to encounter other dogs can do wonders for its socialization. Just remember to correct any negative behavior immediately.

Can Coonhounds Swim? How Can You Train Your Dog to Do So?

It's a myth that all dogs can swim, though most of them can, and the Coonhound is one of them. Mind you, dogs don't look graceful when they do (they aren't swans after all), but that clumsy dog paddle is enough to keep them afloat and to move in the water.

It's actually a good idea to take your dog swimming every once in a while. Swimming will help build their muscles and get them used to the feel of water, which they may have to cross during a hunt.

The important thing for you to remember is to make sure you are always there to supervise it or to pull it to safety, in case of an emergency.

What Happens When You Don't Train Your Coonhound?

Just like with any ability, any skill your Coonhound learned will deteriorate over time, unless you practice with it over and over again. Their learning process is similar to humans; trial and error followed up by constant practice.

Just remember that along with training your Coonhound you have to train yourself to be a good trainer as well. Never forget about trust, positive reinforcement, repetition, patience, and consistency.

CHAPTER 10

Your Coonhound's Diet: What Should It Include?

We have already discussed in a previous chapter that you should consult with a veterinarian about how much to feed your dog taking into account its weight and size, what kind of food you're giving it, how often you feed it, how often its gets exercise, and its metabolic rate.

However, what about the food you can give it?

Treats are an essential part of a dog's training,
but not all of them are good for your dog.

What Else You Can Feed Your Dog

Did you know there are also some human foods that are good for dogs? Here are some of them:

- **Apples** – Slice these into pieces and remove the seeds before feeding to your dog. They have fiber, vitamin A, vitamin C, and also help clean their teeth.
- **Baby Carrots** – These have a lot of fiber, beta carotene, and vitamin A.
- **Cheese** – This is a good source of fat.
- **Cooked Chicken** – This is another good source of protein, use this in place of dog food if you run out.
- **Cooked Oatmeal** – This is a great source of soluble fiber and can also stand in for wheat for dogs with allergies.
- **Peanut Butter** – This is a good source of protein, healthy fats, vitamin B, niacin, and vitamin E.
- **Pumpkin** – Another good source of fiber, beta-carotene, and vitamin A. It's also good for your dog's digestive tract.
- **Salmon** – The real deal has omega-3 fatty acids that keep your dog's coat healthy and shiny.
- **Scrambled Eggs** – Another good source of protein. Raw eggs aren't advisable, though.
- **Yogurt** – A good source of calcium and protein.

Coonhound Treats – Which Ones are Safe to Give?

Treats are an essential part of a dog's training, but not all of them are good for your dog. Avoid giving your dog the following and go for the suggested alternatives instead.

Rawhide bones – This is a popular treat is usually made from the soft inner layer of animals, usually cows. However, before the layer is molded into different shapes, it is also heavily treated with chemicals. This can also cause digestive obstruction.

Use instead: Natural bones like antler.

Chicken strips – While these do contain chicken meat, they also have wheat flour, glycerin, water, sugar, stabilizer, salt, varied kinds of flavoring, preservatives, and artificial colorants.

Use instead: Try giving your dog your own dehydrated treats, you can make them from single ingredient freeze-dried or dehydrated meat.

Dental chews – These are commonly advertised as treats that will feed your dog and clean its teeth at the same time. However, it has ingredients like rice flour, starch, and gum Arabic that aren't good for dogs.

Use instead: Raw, meaty bones or natural recreational bones. You should also brush your dog's teeth regularly (we will discuss more about this in another chapter).

"Salmon" dog treats – Many of these so-called salmon treats don't actually have salmon. They do have salt, flavorings, ascorbyl palmitate, wheat flour, and corn starch that can cause obesity in dogs. They can also contain hydrolyzed poultry protein from meat, considered unfit for human consumption.

Use instead: Try making your own salmon treats using freeze-dried single ingredient salmon or any dehydrated fish.

"Bacon" strips – Despite what others say, bacon is bad for humans. So why give it to dogs? A strip of single bacon begging strip can have ingredients like ground wheat, corn gluten meal, wheat flour, water, glycerin, ground yellow corn, sugar, soybean meal, salt, bacon fat, phosphoric acid, and preservatives like sorbic acid and calcium propionate.

Use instead: Your DIY meat or salmon treats.

This is not to say you shouldn't give your commercial dog treats; there are a lot of good ones out there, just be sure to know what ingredients aren't ideal for dogs.

Also, pet treats shouldn't contain grains, unnecessary fillers, or rendered animal byproducts. Avoid treats that have added sugar in the form of molasses and honey.

How do you know what treats to go for? It helps to go online and see the reviews from dog owners.

The Most Important Thing You Have to Remember About Dog Treats

Dog treats should only be offered as rewards during training exercises. They should not make up a good part of your dog's diet or replace it entirely. In fact, they should only constitute less than 10 percent of your dog's daily food intake.

Overfeeding your dog treats aside from its daily diet will also contribute to its obesity. Don't give your dog treats just because the rest of the family is having snacks, this will remove their purpose as a tool for positive reinforcement.

Are Bones Good for Dogs?

The classic image of the dog will have it resting somewhere with a bone between its teeth, but should you even give your dog a bone in the first place?

The answer is both no and yes.

It's a no if the bones you plan to give them are poultry or pork bones. To begin with, cooked bones have already lost their nutrients during the cooking process. Aside from that, they can splinter into shards and can cause choking aside from posing serious damage to the dog's mouth, throat, or intestines.

It's a yes if you want to give them raw meat bones. In fact, these are the only bones that should be given to a dog, since they still have nutrients in them.

Veterinarians say it's best to give your dog a bone after a meal. Let your dog chew on it for 10 to 15 minutes then take it away and refrigerate it. You can let the dog have it again for the next meal, and totally get rid of it after three or four days.

What to Never Give Your Dog

Just as important as knowing what to give your dog is knowing what to never give it. The following foods can cause severe health problems for dogs, even death. Beware, as some of them are not only foods commonly found in the house, they are also foods you love.

* **Alcohol** – In humans alcohol dulls the senses and coordination by hitting the brain and liver. In dogs it's the same effect, although amplified. Even a small amount of alcohol can cause vomiting, diarrhea, coma, and death.

- **Avocado** – This fruit can be delicious for humans but fatal for dogs, this is because it contains a toxin called persin which can cause breathing difficulties, stomach problems, and fluid buildup in dogs.

- **Chocolate** – Chocolate contains theobromine which can cause vomiting and diarrhea in dogs. It can also cause seizures, in some cases.

- **Coffee and Caffeine** – Same as chocolate, these can cause vomiting, diarrhea, and seizure in dogs. They can also cause abnormal palpitations and long-term damage to a dog's nervous system.

- **Cooked Bones** – For reasons stated above, don't give your dog cooked and small bones.

- **Garlic** – This spice, in whatever form, contains sulfoxides and disulfides that are harmful to your dog's red blood cells. Onions and chives also fall under this category.

- **Grapes and Raisins** – It is not yet known what specific chemical in these foods harms dogs, but if they eat them, even just a little handful, dogs can have serious health problems like liver damage and kidney failure.

- **Macadamia Nuts** – While a handful of grapes and raisins can harm a dog, it takes as little as five macadamia nuts to do the same, particularly, causing muscle tremors, vomiting, rapid breathing and heart rate, increased body temperature, and weakness.

- **Peaches** – Aside from containing pits that can choke a dog, peaches also have amygdalin that has a compound that degrades into hydrogen cyanide, after it is eaten.

- **Pears** – This fruit contains small traces of arsenic that, while not harmful to humans, can be fatal for dogs.
- **Plums** – The pits of this fruit cannot be digested and will stay in a dog's stomach where they can cause intestinal obstruction.
- **Xylitol** – It was mentioned earlier that peanut butter and yogurt can be good for dogs, just remember not to give them products that contain Xylitol, a sweetener that can cause seizures, low blood sugar levels, and death in dogs.
- **Yeast** – Present in almost all dough products like bread and cakes, yeast will expand and rise in your dog's stomach. A little yeast will merely cause mild discomfort, a lot can rupture its stomach and intestines.

These foods can become particularly dangerous if anyone in your family happens to be snacking on them then decides to give the dog some. It's best to make sure everyone in your family knows what the pooches can't eat.

CHAPTER 11

Grooming Your Coonhound: How Can You Make It Easy And Fun?

Yes, Coonhounds like to play in the dust, roll in the dirt, run across streams, and do all the things a dog does. Imagine how they will look after all that! This is why grooming them is important.

Given the popularity of dog grooming shops (not to mention a couple of reality TV shows), it can be forgiven if some people think grooming is limited to just making a dog look pretty. The truth, however, is that grooming isn't just about making a dog look good, it's also taking care of your dog's hygiene, which means taking care of its coat, ears, nails, teeth, etc.

Coonhounds like to play in the dust, roll in the dirt, run across streams, and do all the things a dog does.

Aside from physically, Grooming is also good mentally for your dog as it positively reinforces the bond between dog and owner.

What You Will Need

Bristle Brush – This is for removing dirt from your dog's coat. If you can't find one specifically designed for dogs, a bristle brush for human use will do.

🐾111

Clippers – This is for trimming dogs with long hair.

Comb – Just like the one you have in your dresser, but just make sure this one is exclusively for dog use.

Shedding Blade – This will make it easier for you to remove loose hair on your dog.

Rubber Brush – A brush that has rubber bristles instead of plastic or metal.

Slicker Brush – A brush that has rows of bent bristles, ideal for preventing matting.

Dog Nail Clippers –These are for cutting their nails. Nail clippers for humans shouldn't be used on dogs, because they are shaped the wrong way and their flat edge tends to damage dog claws. Smaller clippers mean better control.

Nail File – These are for filing down the edge of your dog's claws. Nail files for human use will do.

Dog toothpaste – Yes, they do make them, in flavors dogs like, too.

Toothbrush – Again, make sure only the dog uses this.

Dog Treats – For when you have to reward dogs for staying still.

Brushing Your Dog

Why brush? Aside from making your dog feel good, brushing stimulates the natural oils in their skin and removes dead hair and other things in the coat.

Brushing a Long-Haired Dog – Long-haired dogs need more frequent brushing than short-haired ones, so it's advisable to brush them every day.

Start with going over their coat with the slicker brush to remove tangles and dead hair. Make sure you brush all the parts of the dog; head, back, sides, legs, belly, and tail. Be gentle with this brush because it tends to snag on your dog's coat.

Repeat the entire process with the bristle brush. For both brushings brush in the direction the coat naturally settles in.

The clippers don't have to be used in everyday brushing, but for when the dog's hair grows too long, or in the summer, when their coat can cause them to overheat.

Be sure to trim the fur away from their eyes so it will not obstruct their sight, and away from their muzzle so they can eat, drink, or pick up objects without obstruction.

Brushing a Short-Haired Dog – Dogs with shorter hair need less maintenance and can be brushed just once a week. Unlike a long-haired dog, a short-haired one will have fewer tangles in its coat.

Start with a slicker brush, going over all parts of the body. Pull the skin taut before brushing a particular area; this will make it easier to remove dead hair. If there still happens to be a lot of hair on your dog, you should follow this up with the shedding blade.

Make another sweep with a bristle brush or a rubber brush. You can finish up with a fine-tooth comb. Same as with long-haired dogs, their fur will have a natural position where they settle, make sure you follow this position as you comb the hair back in place.

Clipping Your Dog's Nails

Before anything should come the warning that you can seriously injure your dog while clipping their nails. This is because dogs have a vein that runs through their toes. If you cut off too much of a nail it can also cut into that vein. If that happens bleeding will occur, not much to kill the dog outright, but this can cause discomfort and lead to possible complications later on.

Gently separate your dog's toes before clipping the nails. Don't squeeze the toes because it will hurt your dog. Cut their nails as you would your own. Experts recommend getting someone else to help you keep the dog at ease; this is because they can get fidgety particularly when you want them to stay as still as possible.

Note: If you do happen to cut into the vein in the dog's nail you can stop the bleeding by applying a little corn starch on your dog's nail using a cotton swab.

Cleaning Your Dog's Ears

You should clean your dog's ears around once a week, no more than that. Any more or less raises possible infection risks.

Infection from what exactly? Well, everything. The ear canals of dogs are longer and narrower compared to that of humans. This canal (which can vary between 5 to 10 cm long) also has an angled bend, which means things can easily get in, but not out.

You will need the following things to clean your dog's ears: A dog ear cleaning solution and sterile cotton balls. Be sure to do this in a room or location where you don't want things flying around.

Hold your dog or get it in a position where you can easily access its ear and then move the flap of the ear away. Fill the ear canal with the solution; make sure to aim well with the nozzle. After the solution has been applied, massage the skin around your dog's ear to mix the solution with whatever is in the dog's ear.

Release your dog, and by itself, it will shake its head to clear its ears. This motion will remove the mixture from the ear canal. Finish off the job by wiping the opening of your dog's ear canal, until it is dry.

Note: You can also make your own dog ear-cleaning solution by mixing 1-part water and 1-part vinegar mixture. Another recipe is 1-part water, 1-part hydrogen peroxide mixture.

Brushing Your Dog's Teeth

Yes, your dog needs to have its teeth brushed too. Because dogs can't clean their teeth as thoroughly as humans can, this leads to cases of gingivitis or periodontal disease, even in dogs as young as three years of age.

You can brush your dog's teeth the same way you do your own. Toothpaste for dogs is recommended because they will love the taste and there is no risk of poisoning or upset stomach if the dog happens to swallow the toothpaste (a very likely scenario).

Make sure you use a soft-bristle brush, so as not to injure the dog's gums.

Daily brushing of your dog's teeth is recommended.

Bathing Your Dog

You probably know from experience that bathing any dog won't be easy, especially if the dog isn't looking forward to the bath. The image of owners being dragged off, splashed, and wrestled come to mind particularly. The good news is you should only do this once a month.

Get the dog and the supplies you will need ready; in this case dog shampoo and a towel.

Make sure you do this in a bathtub (in which case have a bathmat ready for your dog), or any area where you have full control of the dog; you don't want it running off half-wet tracking water everywhere. If your dog happens to be particularly fidgety, you can start with other parts of the body, not the head immediately.

Wet the dog all over, then apply dog soap. Rub the soap all over your dog, use the occasion to give it a little massage; the dog certainly deserves it. Rinse off the soap then give the dog a drying, with the towel. It will eventually shake on its own to get rid of water, but toweling will help keep the mess to a minimum.

CHAPTER 12

Coonhound Mixes: What Are The Most Common Ones?

Breeding foxhounds and bloodhounds turned out to be a good idea, so some Coonhound owners decided to cross Coonhounds with other breeds to see what results could be achieved. Here are some of the more popular outcomes:

Redbone Coonhound and Poodle Mix – Redbone Coonoodle

It is not known when this mix first arrived; however, it is now a mix familiar with dog lovers. A Redbone Coonoodle will fall between a medium and a large sized dog. Since both parent species are known to be loyal and playful, you can expect the same behavior from it. However, while the Poodle is easy to train, the Redbone Coonoodle can be a little stubborn, like its other ancestor.

Breeding foxhounds and bloodhounds turned out to be a good idea, so some Coonhound owners decided to cross Coonhounds what outcomes would be produced.

Just like a Coonhound, it will see smaller animals as prey, and chase them if they see them. Unlike the Coonhound, it will be satisfied with a level of activity falling in the medium range.

Their major medical concerns include Hip Dysplasia, Eye Disease, Coonhound Paralysis, Addison's Disease, Mitral Valve Disease, and Sebaceous Adenitis.

Both the males and females of this species can reach 18-24 inches in height, and weigh between 45-75 lbs.

Their eye color can either be amber or brown, their noses either black or brown. Their coat, which is wiry, can either be black, white, brown, blue, cream, gray, red, or silver. The coat is usually of above medium length, and at below normal density, and requires weekly brushing.

Black and Tan Coonhound and Poodle Mix – Black and Tan Coonoodle

This breed isn't considered mature until three years old; that's good news for some and bad news for others. This mix isn't just playful; some owners have described their dogs as sometimes acting goofy. However, this dog is also described as having an air of poise that offsets its silly nature.

This dog is also smart and easy to train, but its memory is also so good it can hold on to bad habits or pre-training knowledge.

Their major health issues include Gastric Torsion, Hip Dysplasia, Addison's Disease, and Cushing's Disease.

Males of this species can be 22-25 inches high and weigh 50-70 lbs. Females can be 22-23 inches high and weigh 50 to 60 lbs.

In appearance, a Black and Tan Coonoodle will have brown eyes, a black nose, and a wavy coat of above normal density and medium-length hair. Colors can vary from black, fawn, white, gray, silver, brown, and cream.

Redbone Coonhound Labrador Mix

The result of the breeding between these two breeds is a large dog, either looking more like a Coonhound or more like a

Labrador by chance. Just like both its ancestors, it's a dog that requires a lot of physical activity. It will want to be outside playing with a frisbee or running around in the dog park. The absence of physical activity can cause it to be rather destructive around the house.

While its Labrador ancestor is very friendly, this breed has been described as a bit reserved around strangers. That said, they are very affectionate with people they already know, relishing in their company and eager to please them.

Their major health issues include Hip Dysplasia, Elbow Dysplasia, and heart problems. Eye health may also become a concern. However, despite being what is called a designer breed, the good news is this breed is not known to develop medical issues that persist through their lifetime.

Both males and females can be 22-24 inches high and weigh between 55-65 lbs. This breed will have a red-gold coat of short, coarse fur.

Boxer/Treeing Walker Coonhound Mix – BT Walker

The result of mixing these breeds is a dog that can fall between a medium to large size, with more noticeable features of its Boxer heritage; strong facial features and large paws, although it has also been described as having the elegant look of the Treeing Walker.

Because both its ancestors are very active dogs, this breed is also designed for a lot of physical activity. It will want to be outside and chasing things, most of the time. They can be stubborn, which means training for socialization at an early age is recommended. They can also be territorial and fiercely protective of their loved ones.

Their major health concerns include Cardiomyopathy, Subvalvular Aortic Stenosis, Degenerative Myelopathy, and Corneal Dystrophy.

The eyes of this breed are brown, the nose is black. They have a very dense coat of short hair that can be either brown, red, or white. While their coat is easy to take care of, they do shed a lot and brushing them daily is advisable.

The males of this species can grow 20-27 inches high and between 50-75 lbs. the females are about as tall but weigh only between 50 to 60 lbs.

English Bull/Treeing Walker Coonhound Mix

A dog bred from both these breeds will more closely resemble his Treeing Walker ancestor, with a lean, muscular body, as opposed to the chunkiness of the English Bull. Unlike other Coonhound mixes, this breed actually doesn't require familiarization to become friends with other dogs and other kinds of animals. Despite the fearsome reputation of its ancestor, it can also be quite good-natured and can be raised around young children.

Like its ancestor, it also enjoys a lot of physical activity, and it is recommended you give it 45 minutes up to an hour of intense playtime each day.

This breed is usually very healthy and poses no major health issues, although it is known to suffer from Entropion, Cherry Eye, and certain types of dog allergies.

In appearance, this breed will almost exclusively have brown eyes, a dark nose, and a coat of straight hair that is below medium length and above normal in density. The color of the coat is either red, fawn, brindle, or a tri-color combination.

Both the males and females of the species can be between 15-25 inches in height and weight between 50-70 lbs.

Bluetick Coonhound/Poodle Mix – Bluetick Coonoodle

Off all the Coonhound mixes, the Bluetick Coonoodle is said to be the most laid back; it will not get excited until its hunting instincts kick in. But underneath this seemingly calm veneer, the Bluetick Coonoodle also inherited something from its Poodle ancestor; the characteristic of being high-strung.

This will manifest itself when being introduced the first time to strangers, children, or other animals, so it is best if there is someone it trusts to make these introductions. It is also advisable for them to be trained in socialization at an early age. However, after it has become familiar with someone, the affection will start to be reciprocated, and it will become a lovable dog.

Their potential major health issues include Sebaceous Adenitis, Bloat, and Addison's Disease.

In appearance, this dog will have brown eyes, a black nose, and wavy, dense hair of above medium length all over its body. Its color can either be blue, black, white, silver, gray, cream, or brown.

The males of this species can grow up to 21-30 inches tall and weigh between 55-85 lbs. The females can grow up to 15-28 inches tall and weigh between 45-65 lbs.

Treeing Walker/Poodle mix – Treeing Walker Coonoodle

A Treeing Walker Coonoodle can look like either a Poodle or a Treeing Walker Coonhound, nothing really in-between. The look of this dog's face has also been described to vary between the appearance of these two species. What is consistent is that the snout and muzzle of this dog is medium to short in length.

While known to be friendly, this breed has also been known to be mischievous and can even get rough playing with children it is already familiar with, so supervision by an adult is always recommended if you want them to play with the kids. Like its ancestors, this breed also wants a lot of intense outdoor activities.

Their major potential health concerns are Eye Disease, Addison's Disease, and Corneal Dystrophy.

In appearance, this dog will have either brown or amber eyes and either a black or brown nose. Its hair is wavy, and it will have an above medium-length coat in normal density throughout its body. The color of the coat is either brindle, sable, white, silver, fawn, Isabella, cream, red, brown, gray, or black.

The males of this species can grow from 17-27 inches in height and weigh between 48-80 lbs. The females can grow from 15-25 inches in height and weigh between 45-75 lbs.

You may have noticed many breeders decided to mix Coonhounds with poodles, quite often. This is because, although the Poodle is more familiar as a show dog, it was actually bred as a working dog. In France, the larger standard poodles were used for hunting ducks, while the smaller ones were used to sniff out truffles in the woods.

Mini Coonhounds – What Are They?

Don't be fooled by the name. Yes, they are cute, but these small designer hybrids that look like small Black and Tan Coonhounds have no Coonhound blood whatsoever.

It's all in the appearance, says breed creator Wallace Havens.

"The Mini Coonhound is a new hybrid that looks like the old Black and Tan Coonhound people use to hunt coon with. The big difference is, these mature at 10-20 lbs. and have no Coonhound in them," Havens says.

He adds that the following breeds were used to develop the mini Coonhound; the shorthaired Chihuahua, the Italian Greyhound, the Rat Terrier, the Beagle, and the Min Pin. Beyond that information, the percentage of the breeds used in this mix, or if there were other breeds included, is unknown.

While these little dogs look like the real thing, they don't act like the Coonhounds and have no drive to hunt game. Wallace himself said the dogs were not bred to hunt but to be comfy home animals.

"We breed them for the retired hunter that wants a dog around that reminds him of the old days. His wife may not want a big Coonhound in the house, so the Mini Coonhound is the perfect little look-alike and is bred specially for a family pet. People will love this little dog with big ears. They make excellent little 'tree dogs' and will be good with kids if trained correctly. No professional groomer required in their upkeep," Havens concludes.

CHAPTER 13

Hunting With The Coonhound: How To Live and Love This Experience?

N ow that you have a well-trained Coonhound eager for some action, it's time to go hunting, right? Wait a minute, hold your horses…or in this case, your hounds. The America of the frontier days is no more after all, and while the America of today is just full of trees and game, it is also full of hunting rules and regulations.

While the US government does have the United State Fish and Wildlife Service to manage wildlife in the country, the government also gave its states free rein over regulations involving hunting with dogs. With each state free to legislate as it pleases, the rules regarding hunting with dogs vary per state.

If you don't want your Coonhound taken away from you it's important you know what the rules are where you live. Your Coonhound's life may depend on it.

For example, in Alaska, a state park officer may seize a dog running at large in a state park if it is harassing the wildlife.

In Colorado, owners of dogs that happen to kill small game, birds, or mammals will be prosecuted and charged the value of each animal killed.

In Montana, dogs are allowed to chase off predators that kill livestock but are not allowed to chase game animals.

The harshest appears to be in New York, where anyone, not just state employees or park personnel, can kill a dog while it is pursuing or killing the game in protected areas, without fear of prosecution.

The most lenient appears to be Georgia, where killing a raccoon, fox, opossum, or bobcat will not be punishable by law (but hunting deer with hunting dogs is).

In Arkansas, it is also illegal for state employees to stop dogs from running at large since recreational hunting has been ruled good for wildlife management.

State Park Rules

Almost all states ban the presence of pets in state parks. However, there are a few exceptions.

In Delaware, North Dakota, Oklahoma Oregon, Pennsylvania, Rhode Island, South Carolina, South Dakota, Tennessee, Texas, Vermont, Washington, West Virginia, Wisconsin, and Wyoming dogs are allowed only in certain areas of state parks and they must be on a leash that is six feet long (182 cm) or less.

Ohio and Utah also require this but have the additional requirement that owners be able to present proof of rabies vaccination, upon request.

In Virginia, dogs are allowed in other state parks, but not the Back Bay National Wildlife Refuge.

If you don't want your Coonhound taken away from you it's important you know what the rules are where you live. Your Coonhound's life may depend on it.

For a complete list of regulations regarding dogs chasing wildlife, you can check out the website listed in our bonus chapter.

What About Raccoons?

It was for these animals that Coonhounds were bred in the first place. Is hunting them legal in the US?

We know a lot about the Coonhounds, but almost nothing about the raccoon itself. Are they still as destructive, as they were during the days of the early settlers? The answer is yes.

This is because raccoons are omnivorous; they will eat almost anything from different types of fruits, berries, nuts, acorns, to animals like fish, crayfish, frogs, snails, turtles, birds, and even small mammals like mice, muskrats, and rabbits. They will also go for garbage and your groceries.

Raccoons mainly breed in February or March, and it takes 63 days before a litter of three to five kits is born. They are weaned between two and four months of age but open their eyes as early as three weeks old.

Their intelligence and dexterous paws make them the perfect opportunistic predator, they are able to scale fences, break into chicken coops, open trash bins, and even sneak into houses using the chimney in search of food.

Raccoons are also accredited to the rise of rabies in the wild; they are identified as the major wildlife host of this disease.

Raccoon Hunting

So, is hunting raccoon legal in the US? While raccoons are considered protected animals, they are also considered furbearers, meaning their fur has a variety of uses. In some states, there are established seasons for running, hunting, and trapping raccoons. You also need to have a permit to do so, and you will be subject to certain bag limits.

For example, in Tennessee raccoon hunting season begins in mid-September and ends in February, with the bag limit of one raccoon per hunter per day. In Kentucky, there is no bag limit, but their season begins in October and ends on the last day of February.

In Iowa, you need a hunting license before you can even train Coonhounds, and then a trapping license to hunt raccoons.

During months not considered part of the hunting season, treeing a raccoon for sport but leaving it alive is considered legal.

Pest Control

Most states have provisions for property owners seeking to control raccoons that are destroying their crops, livestock, and property. However, it is advised to check with the local wildlife agency before taking any action, just to be sure.

What if a raccoon gets stuck in your attic, basement, or any part of your house? Do you have to get any clearance with your local wildlife agency? Do you have to wait until certain months to act? In this case no; any property owner is authorized to trap a nuisance animal in his residence.

Modern Raccoon Hunts

These days there are other venues a modern Coonhound hunter can go to let his dogs hunt coon. He can enter his dog into a number of coon hunting competitions called "nite hunts," sanctioned by the different kennel clubs and hunting associations in the US.

The American Kennel Club hosts an average of 60 nite hunts a year, along with their regular bench show, water race, and field trial events.

The American Coon Hunters' Association has also hosted hunts, their largest of which is the Grand American Coon Hunt, which has been held in Orangeburg, South Carolina, since 1965. The hunt has a special event, where children who own Coonhounds can participate.

However, the largest coon hunting event is hosted by the United Kennel Club, which sanctioned over 6,000 such events across the US in 2002 alone. The biggest of these Coonhound events are part of the Autumn Oaks, Leafy Oaks, and Coonhunting World Championships.

The Autumn Oaks event, already mentioned in a previous chapter, attracts competitors from all over the US and Canada.

In addition to hunts where any breed of Coonhound can join, the UKC also holds a number of nite hunts each year, limited to specific breeds of Coonhounds.

Coonhunting Terminology

So, you want to get into the world of coonhunting? Then you have to familiarize yourself with the following terms:

- **Babbler.** A dog that constantly opens even when no track is evident.
- **Backtrack.** A dog that runs a track in the wrong direction.
- **Barks Per Minute.** Amount of barks counted during each minute of treeing.
- **Breaking Scent.** The scent of unwanted game that is used to break a dog from pursuing unwanted game.
- **Cast.** A group of four handlers and four dogs competing in a nite hunt.
- **Check-in.** A dog that will come back in if no game is found.
- **E-Collar.** An electronic collar used in the training of hounds. A shock collar is used for breaking dogs from running unwanted game.
- **Gator.** A dog that frequently fights with other dogs.
- **Junk Game.** Any unwanted game (also called trash and off-game).
- **Open.** Refers to the action of a dog barking on trial.
- **Pup Trainer.** An older dog that is hunted with a young pup to help teach and train that pup.
- **Scratched.** Dogs that are "scratched" are eliminated from a hunt.
- **Shining.** The act of searching a tree with lights to find the raccoon.
- **Slick Tree.** When the dog trees a tree that has no game (also called an Empty Tree).
- **Split Tree.** When dogs tree on separate trees from one another, it is referred to as being split treed.

- **Strike.** When the dog barks or opens when it smells a track.
- **Tracking Collar.** A collar that is used for locating a hound. Some are equipped with a tree switch to let you know if the dog is treed.
- **Treed.** When the dog is at the tree with game in it and barking.

Both the UKC and the AKC will scratch a dog for aggression, as well as fighting with other dogs.

To adopt a more humane stance regarding raccoons, dogs and their handlers are discouraged from harming or killing hunted raccoons. Harming or killing it will be declared misconduct, and result in deductions.

CHAPTER 14
Conclusion

Coonhounds have come a long way since their early days as mere animals bred to deal with vermin, pests, and threats to the early colonists, who came to North America from the UK and Europe. Now more than just hunters and protectors, they are also show dogs, service dogs, and most importantly, beloved family pets.

While the physical characteristics of the breed itself have changed quite a bit throughout the centuries, it is their nature that has remained the same; their drive to stay active, their stubbornness and determination, their fierce loyalty to their pack, their need to be loved, and their desire to be close to their owners.

Coonhounds have come a long way since their early days as mere animals bred to deal with vermin, pests, and threats to the early colonists.

If you have come this far and you are still determined to get and successfully raise one, then congratulations; it seems you have the stubbornness and determination of a Coonhound as well.

With that said, it will not easy to raise a Coonhound; you have to be able to provide it wide open spaces for running around and playing in, you have to devote a lot of time in exercising and caring for your Coonhound, you have to be familiar with what is good and bad for them, and what translates to proper or improper behavior.

You also have to be able to tell when your Coonhound is unwell, what is ailing it, and what you should do about these ailments.

Another thing you must never forget is while you did buy or adopt that Coonhound and it is your property, dogs are living breathing creatures with feelings. They will get excited at the sight of prey, they feel exhilarated during exercise, they feel shame when you scold them, and they will long for you when you aren't with them.

For you, a Coonhound may just be a companion for a short time, but for the dog, you are a companion for life.

Yes, we can promise you the task of raising and caring for a Coonhound will be challenging; it will be full of struggles, trials, and tears (the ones from your face and the ones on the couch, the dog toys, the wallpaper, the carpet, your clothes, etc.). However, we can also promise you that the entire experience will be a rewarding one that, in the end, will give you one of the most loyal, affectionate, and amazing creatures Nature can provide.

We wish you the best of luck in this endeavor.

Your Trusted Coonhound Resource List

Coonhound Breeders in the USA

- Puppies whelped from a champion Coonhound
  https://www.oakhillkennel-deer.com/american-black-and-tan-Coonhound/
- Breeders who believe Coonhounds should be more than show dogs
  http://www.grandriverredbones.com/
- Breeders that specialize on old-style Bluetick pedigree
  http://www.evenstarhounds.com/
- American BT resource center
  https://www.facebook.com/BTCoonhoundClub/
- A breeder based in Illinois
  http://www.saltcreekch.com/
- A breeder specializing in TW Coonhounds
  http://www.roanokeriverkennels.com/
- A kennel that specializes in different Coonhound breeds
  http://coldcreekkennels.webstarts.com/

- A Utah-based Coonhound breeder
  http://www.wheelerhounds.com/
- Breeders that takes pride in producing intelligent Plott hounds
  http://www.fourcountycornersplotts.com/
- A breeder based in Washington State
  http://sandyriversknl.tripod.com/
- A breeder that specializes in Blueticks
  http://krautcreek.tripod.com/
- A breeder that specializes in BT Coonhounds
  http://www.angelfire.com/ar2/blackandtans/
- A Coonhound breeder based in Iowa
  http://www.eglisblackandtans.com/
- A Texas-based Coonhound breeder
  http://www.whitedeerpreserve.com/
- A breeder specializing in TW Coonhounds
  http://triplejkennel.yolasite.com/

Coonhound Breeders in the UK

- BT breeders based in the UK
  https://www.covehitheCoonhounds.co.uk/
- A breeder based in Nottinghamshire
  https://www.blackandtanCoonhounds.co.uk/about
- A local site that advertises available Coonhounds for purchase
  http://www.localpuppybreeders.co.uk/black-and-tan-Coonhound-puppies-for-sale-in-the-uk/

- Another local site that advertises available Coonhounds https://topdogconeyisland.com/250-american-english-Coonhound-puppies-for-sale-uk.html
- A breeder that specializes in BT Coonhounds http://debbiejay.co.uk/

Coonhound Breeders in Australia

- The only BT Coonhound breeder recognized by the Dogs Victoria Association https://dogsvictoria.org.au/family-pet/dogs-and-puppies/buying-a-puppy/breed-information-and-registered-breeders/black-and-tan-Coonhound/
- A site that advertises Coonhounds for sale https://www.dogzonline.com.au/breeds/breeders/bluetick-Coonhound.asp

These websites can help you find the right Coonhound for you

- https://www.petfinder.com/
- https://www.adoptapet.com/

Official Websites of the UKC, AKC, and ACHA

- http://worldhunt.org/
- https://www.akc.org/
- https://www.ukcdogs.com/

Coonhound Rescue Groups

- https://www.houndsong.com/
- http://neCoonhoundrescue.org/Home_Page.html
- https://www.carolinaCoonhoundrescue.com/index.html

This website run by the American Black and Tan Coonhound Rescue will help you find Black and Tans specifically:

- http://www.Coonhoundrescue.com/rescuedogs.html

This group of Coonhound rescuers based in Ontario is continuously on the lookout for foster home providers:

- https://www.Coonhoundrescue.ca/

List of Plants Poisonous for Dogs

- https://www.aspca.org/pet-care/animal-poison-control/toxic-and-non-toxic-plants

American Association of Poison Control Center

- https://www.aapcc.org/

State Regulations for Hunting with Dogs

- https://www.animallaw.info/article/table-state-and-federal-laws-concerning-dogs-chasing-wildlife

UKC and AKC Rulebook on Coonhunting Events and Nite Hunts

* https://www.ukcdogs.com/docs/hunting/Coonhound-rulebook.pdf
* http://images.akc.org/pdf/rulebooks/RE9ACH.pdf

News About Coonhounds

* https://kstp.com/news/fight-duke-coon-hound-east-bethel-could-head-court/4716028/
* http://www.startribune.com/after-losing-duke-east-bethel-family-takes-dogfight-to-city-hall/475938003/
* https://www.indystar.com/story/life/2014/08/27/Coonhound-convention-taking-over-richmond/14622421/

www.ingramcontent.com/pod-product-compliance
Lightning Source LLC
Chambersburg PA
CBHW072155090426
42740CB00012B/2268